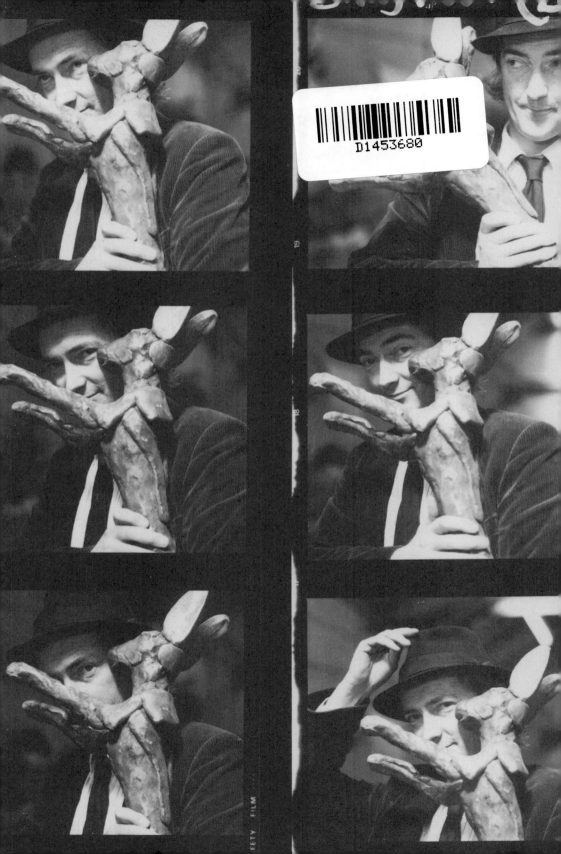

# WITH BARRY FLANAGAN

TRAVELS THROUGH
TIME AND SPAIN

Self Portrait, 1981,
Charcoal and
watercolour on paper,
15" x 10 ½" / 38.1cm
x 26.7cm

# WITH BARRY FLANAGAN

## TRAVELS THROUGH TIME AND SPAIN

RICHARD McNEFF

THE LILLIPUT PRESS

ALSO BY RICHARD McNEFF

*Sybarite among the Shadows*
*Poems of Martin Watson Todd* (Editor)

First published 2012 by

# THE LILLIPUT PRESS LTD

62–63 Sitric Road, Arbour Hill, Dublin 7, Ireland
www.lilliputpress.ie

ISBN 978 1 84351 322 3

1 3 5 7 9 10 8 6 4 2

Set in 12 on 15pt Perpetua
Design by Niall McCormack
Printed and bound in England by MPG Books, Bodmin, Cornwall

OPPOSITE
Ubu sketch, 1974,
3 ⁷/₁₆" x 5 ¼" /
8.8cm x 13.4cm

*For Mandana*

زنهار ز جام می مرا قوت کنید
وین چهرهٔ کهربا چو یاقوت کنید
چون مرده شوم بباده شوئید مرا
وز چوب رزم تختهٔ تابوت کنید

From *The Rubáiyát of Omar Khayyám*

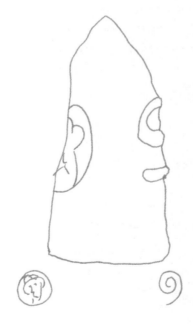

# ACKNOWLEDGMENTS

This book would not have been published without the help and input of Jo Melvin (the Estate of Barry Flanagan) and Vivienne Guinness, and I would like to thank the following for their encouragement: Enrique Juncosa, Oengus MacNamara, Sarah Munn, Robert Nurden, Tony Peake, Elena Ruiz Sastre, Jessica Sturgess, Kevin Whitney; and at the foundry, Henry Abercrombie ('Ab'), Jerry Hughes and Mark Jones. I thank Antonio Colinas for permission to use his poem 'Head of the Goddess in my Hands' ('Cabeza de la diosa entre mis manos') and Helga Watson Todd for permission to reproduce 'Games', a poem by her late husband Martin Watson Todd. I thank Miquel Barceló for allowing the use of his portrait of Barry Flanagan. Thanks also to Djinn von Noorden for her assistance with the editing and Antony Farrell at The Lilliput Press.

# PHOTO CREDITS

The Estate of Barry Flanagan courtesy Plubronze Limited
Hugh Gordon
Mark Jones
Vivienne Guinness
Gaudier Deblonde
Kevin Scanlan
Hugh Lane City Gallery
Andre Morin

Some time ago There was a 2 man show
with Marcel … And it has always bothered
me that Ibiza Museum was considered not
worthy to be notified in the stream of events.
It was curated by Richard McNeff
& to know about it would be a propper [*sic*] thing.

(Email from Barry Flanagan to Galerie Lelong, Paris,
25 November 2008)

# PREFACE

What follows is an account of time spent with Barry Flanagan from 1987, when we first met, to 2009 when he sadly passed away. This account focuses especially on the exhibition he put on at the Museum of Contemporary Art of Ibiza in 1992, which we then took to Palma, Mallorca, as well as describing his interests in Madrid, Barcelona and England. Most of these doings have been bypassed in the standard chronologies. This work has been undertaken in order to rectify this, and to give an insight into a remarkable man and artist.

1

HALF AN HOUR after leaving Palma, the mountains of
the west coast of Mallorca rose before us. Barry was at the wheel
of the hire car, staring fixedly at the steepening road ahead, which
was lined on either side by ever-taller hills. Still embarrassed by the
nervousness the traffic of the unfamiliar city had induced in me and
by my reluctance to drive, I now offered to take the wheel whenever
Barry wished.

'I'd rather stick with it if you don't mind,' the sculptor
responded.

We carried on ascending through a landscape that was now
mountainous and exhilarating. I could not understand why Barry was
applying all his concentration to the unfolding road and ignoring such
spectacular views. In the end I asked him.

'I find being dwarfed by mountains unsettling,' he explained.

'The opposite of vertigo,' I suggested, and then one of us coined
the word 'invertigo' to describe this.

It was the first time that morning we had laughed. Thinking
about it later, however, the words tallied with something Monica,

the sculptor's mother, had told me. Barry had been born in 1941, a year after his father Bill's employer, Warner Brothers, had arranged the evacuation of his two older brothers and elder sister to North America.

'If you want to understand Barry,' Monica had said, 'you have to realize he was the centre of attention until he was five. Then suddenly Patsy, Mike and John came back and grabbed all the limelight. He never got over it.'

This was a key to Barry's nature: a keen resentment of being dwarfed by mountains, older siblings or anything or anybody else for that matter. This led him to raise himself through work and deed, until he became a sort of giant. Allied to this was his hatred of being ignored, patronized or taken for granted. Any one of these transgressed the 'civility' he was so fond of citing and could provoke the storm he was to warn me at my peril to avoid.

: : : : : : : : : : : : : : : :

I first saw Barry at a wedding reception at Es Figueral on the north coast of Ibiza in 1987, the year he moved to the island. I was there because Kika, my partner, had been invited by Renate, Barry's partner. Barry was wearing a shabby blue-grey denim suit and a cap, which resembled those worn by ticket inspectors on East European trains. He had an alert fine-featured face, hair just starting to silver at the back and sides, and a face speckled with freckles. Kika told me he was an artist and I assumed he must be another skint bohemian drawn to the island by its congenial climate, tolerant locals and, in those pre-Euro days, hospitable prices. It was only later I heard on the bush telegraph that Barry was actually a figure with an international reputation, an artist-star in our meteor-filled sky. He had met Renate in London, running into her in Cork Street when she was an art student. They had had a son together, Alfred, and then moved to Ibiza where Renate's parents had been living for several years. Annabelle, their daughter, was born on Ibiza. Barry delivered her himself.

I did not talk with Barry that day but registered him as a vague figure on the fringe of things, much how I felt myself. A little while later he came to a reading some friends and I were giving in a laundrette in San Juan. He spoke to me afterwards and seemed

quite animated by the passages from a work in progress I had read to the audience. I found it difficult to understand what he was saying. Nevertheless, the fact he had liked what he heard may explain my next encounter with him, a few days before Christmas, when two bottles appeared on Kika's table at the Royalty, the main café in Santa Eulalia. Their origin was a mystery: Kika had gone to the ladies and found them waiting for her on her return. The consensus was that Barry was the source. His generosity, particularly in the provision of food and drink, was already passing into legend. One bottle was of Hennessy Cognac, the other a fine Russian vodka. We took them home and drank most of their contents in the company of two friends.

Kika was tall and slender, sometimes worryingly so. She was a great beauty, fêted in the carousel of Ibiza nightlife, until one winter she was flung off and went on the slide. She had the soul of a clown and sometimes dressed as one. One day when she was sick, I met Barry in town and he came back with me to the house to visit her. He had a small sketchbook with him and sat down by the bed and immediately began drawing her profile. He was using a pen and as was usual for him the nib hardly ever left the sheet of paper as he traced her straight nose and prominent lips with an uninterrupted line. His shoulders were hunched as he worked and the furious concentration that possessed him made me wonder if there was something shamanic in this act: it was as though by sketching he hoped to draw out her pain. When he had finished, he tore the sheet out and gave it to her.

At this time I was renting a house about a mile along the coast from Santa Eulalia at a place called Niu Blau. A creek separated the house from a snug, pine-shaded beach where there was a restaurant, whose owner, Juanito, was my landlord. The house had three tiny rooms, a kitchen and a shower. A path came up from the creek and made a right angle, running past the house and then alongside the forest in front of it. At night the only sound was the sea, the ebb and flow of waves that lulled you to sleep. There was a porch outside and a small garden I had made of geraniums, roses and jasmine, which was divided by a path of pebbles gathered from the beach. The geraniums blossomed through the year.

Niu Blau meant the Blue Nest in Ibicenco, and had been the name given to his studio by Rigoberto Soler, an artist who painted there in the 1930s. One Sunday we had a visit from Barry and Renate. It was a windy day, and leaving the ladies in the house, the sculptor and I went for a stroll up along the path to the headland. There was a crumbling wall of reddish stone to one side behind which lived Mariano, the old fisherman, in a house that was formerly a boat shed. Further up, in a splendidly located but simple house, whose erection would be forbidden today by the Law of Coasts, dwelt an affable if slightly cantankerous American, who was one of the founding fathers of the foreign community on Ibiza and had run a school on the island in the 1960s. We visited neither of them but instead observed the way strong gusts from the choppy sea were bending the trees along the coast.

'You know what's happening, don't you?' said Barry.

The sea was rough, the wind was high, that much I was aware of.

'The wind is baffled by the pines.'

Barry explained this in a stilted way that did not seem to invite reply. This, coupled with a growing awe I felt for him, made me silent, a state difficult for me as I am by nature garrulous, uncomfortable with pauses and duty-bound to break them. Barry was wearing a green corduroy jacket, baggy tweed trousers and a collarless striped shirt. There was jerkiness to his movements and at one point he turned and took in the salty air through flared nostrils, looking very much the hare as he did so. I was intrigued by him and by his visit, wondering if it had been inspired by anything more than Renate and Kika's friendship. It had.

'I have a commission for you,' Barry declared when the four of us were back in the tiny sitting room. We were drinking the last of the Hennessy (I was too abashed to ask if it had come from him). 'I wish you to produce a piece of writing. The subject matter and deadline are entirely of your choosing.'

I was at that time working on an historical novel, which had been triggered by a remark I had come across in a book by a Spanish writer about the Balearic islands. According to L. Pericot Garcia, the Romans had looked on Ibiza as the setting for a 'sweet and honeyed life', or *la dolce vita* as we call it today. Just as now, so in the first century AD there had been a raffish, hedonistic community composed of rich expatriates, criminals and artists.

In order to supply background, I used to go to the small municipal library in Ibiza town and research the history of the island in antiquity, drawing mainly from the work of a priest and antiquarian called Isidor Macabich. I read accounts of how the Greeks who fought at Troy had been shipwrecked on the beaches of Ibiza and lived out their days entirely naked, perfecting their sling-throwing skills. The Phoenicians had populated the island, establishing the city of Ibiza in 654 BC, and the island's name probably derived from a war god called Bes. It seemed a simple matter to put my research notes together, type them into something resembling a coherent text, and call this 'The Island of Bes'. The next time Kika saw Renate in town she mentioned that the commission was ready. The following Sunday Barry showed up at the house with Flan, the flame-haired daughter of his first marriage, in tow. I handed him the piece, which I had typed out on my old Olivetti. It consisted of five A4 sheets of double-spaced text. Barry perused it with great concentration for a few minutes. Then he turned to me and, with a sharp, not particularly friendly expression on his face, asked me what I wanted for it.

I knew commission meant money, and the word was the key to most of Barry's dealings. I had made almost nothing from a writing career that up to that time had spanned twenty years; indeed, if you factored in postage and ink, the balance was firmly in the red. On the other hand, life on Ibiza then was cheap and time-friendly, and the money[1] I made from teaching added up to just enough to pay the rent, run an old banger, dawdle in the sun drinking coffee and eat numerous *menus del día*. It seemed churlish to cadge money for something that had been a pleasure, not a chore.

'I want you to have it,' I grandly declared. 'We are fellow artists and money should not be an issue.'

'So you don't want anything,' said Barry by way of confirmation, in a tone that implied he was not as happy as I expected with this arrangement.

I thought no more about it until I ran into him in Pomelo's, a bar frequented by expats beside the new market in Santa Eulalia. He was drinking whisky and water from a tall glass at the bar. I went and joined him, noticing the liver spots dotted across his hand as he swirled the liquid round in the glass. I ordered a *carajillo* for myself (a small black coffee with brandy).

'I am sorry you saw fit to refuse my commission,' he announced. He then reached into the inner pocket of his jacket, drew out a brown leather wallet and extracted two pristine ten-thousand peseta[1] notes of the new blue variety. 'Robin, however, has shown me the courtesy of accepting it. Would you be so good as to give this to him?'

I was too stung to say anything. Feeling foolish, I took the money and did indeed deliver it to Robin, who was living in a house not far from my own between the Es Canar and San Carlos roads. Apart from being aspiring writers, Robin and I had a lot in common, having first bumped into each other in the underground scene centred round the psychedelic heartlands of Portobello Road and the Roundhouse, Chalk Farm, in the late 1960s. It was quite common for me to come across people I had known from that time on Ibiza or meet others linked to it. Along with Goa and Amsterdam, the island was still one of the key bastions of the hippies' last stand, a Bermuda Triangle in which dreams and ideals were vanishing by the planeload.

Robin knew Barry had commissioned me as well. We were in a race, but I had never heard the starting gun.

'Barry likes games,' Robin said. 'He's playing one with you. Don't you see what he's trying to tell you?'

I had some inkling. 'To be a bit more businesslike,' I ventured, 'and forget all this wishy-washy, brother-artist stuff.'

'Precisely,' said Robin.

'I could stomach that, but giving me the dosh to give to you is really rubbing my nose in it.'

'It will make your nose harder,' said Robin.

Some time later another interpretation of Barry's action suggested itself. Through not playing by his rules, I had robbed him of control and this was something he did not like. Before moving to Ibiza

[1] During the time covered by this account there was considerable fluctuation in the value of the peseta in relation to the pound. For the purposes of simplicity, the rate used throughout is £1 = 200 pesetas.

he had lost his driving licence for a while and been forced to employ a driver. He had the car modified, however, so the horn was moved to the passenger side. He had no compunction about using it and did so frequently, sometimes in traffic jams, narrowly avoiding a fight with the occupant of the car in front on one occasion. It was his way of staying in charge. Barry gave his driver one of his most remarkable bronzes, *Vessel, In Memoriam* (1981). The driver did not know what to do with it and gave it to his mother. Barry frequently gave work away on the spur of the moment, often to people like drivers or pub-keepers who had little notion of their artistic or financial worth.

This reinforces the likelihood that his reaction to my gift was about control, not the need for artists to behave like businessmen.

Notwithstanding this insight nor the conversation I had had with Robin, my resentment did not fade and when a day or so later I saw Barry get out of his car outside the Cruz del Sur building in Santa Eulalia, where he kept a flat, I decided to accost him. He seemed surprised to see me and gave me a half smile.

'I thought you should know that I gave the money to Robin.'

'Good.' He nodded as though this was a perfectly acceptable state of affairs.

'How could you take advantage of my goodwill like that?' I demanded.

He leaned his head to one side and his eyes narrowed as though appraising me for a bust.

'The shape of your heads is different!' he declared, as though that explained everything.

There were a couple of postscripts. One concerned an artist's model called Eileen Fox, universally known as Foxy, who had moved to Ibiza a few years before. A short dark woman with liberal mounds of flesh, Foxy had modelled for Francis Bacon as well as Barry and had been a well-known character around Soho, celebrated in a rather scurrilous anecdote by Jeffrey Bernard concerning firemen and a hose for which she frequently considered suing him. Foxy and I shared a birthday and had thrown a few memorable parties together. She had also supplied Kika and me with the first house we had together in an urbanization near Santa Gertrudis by simply passing on the keys she had received from the Ibicenco landlord and presenting us as de facto tenants. She sat for Barry again and from this he produced a work in crayon on paper called *Old Woman in Soho* (1989), in which Foxy's elephantine proportions seem to anticipate those of the model in Lucien Freud's more celebrated 1995 painting, *Benefits Supervisor Sleeping*. Foxy also inspired a small rounded fertility-like object in clay based on the Venus of Willendorf, a Palaeolithic statuette with huge breasts and abdomen found in Lower Austria[2]. Barry called his creation *Bes*. In my piece, of course, Bes had been a god but this was a minor detail.

The second postscript began in the Virgin Megastore, then at the end of Oxford Street, while I was visiting London that summer.

[2] The magazine from the sculpture department of St Martin's showed a photograph of the figurine cradled in William Tucker's hand – the carving was revered amongst sculptors.

I noticed an anthology of transgressive writing with the famous photograph of Aldous Huxley parting a thin curtain that symbolized the doors of perception on the cover. The book was called *Rapid Eye* and was a compendium of writings that had appeared in a magazine of the same name, chiefly work by counter-cultural writers such as William Burroughs and Alexander Trocchi. Vaguely resentful that my own alternative scribbling had never appeared in such tomes, I opened the anthology and found my name misspelled at the top of the page. This was above a story called 'Sybarite Among the Shadows', which had first appeared in *International Times* (also known as *IT*), the underground newspaper, in 1977. The story described a meeting between Aldous Huxley and Aleister Crowley in Nazi Berlin, in which they took mescaline together. Derived from a questionable anecdote in a book on ritual magic, it has enjoyed an interesting shelf life since publication, being pirated and published in Russian as well as quoted as irrefutable fact in books of the history as conspiracy variety.

I arranged to meet the publisher and editor in Brighton. They were apologetic but had tried to contact me when they had first republished the story in the original magazine. They seemed vaguely miffed that I expected some money, pointing out that William Burroughs had supplied his piece for no more than a bottle of red wine. I had learned my lesson, however, and was hard-nosed and businesslike, extracting two hundred pounds in the process.

A few months later I had a letter from the editor, the late Simon Dwyer. They were producing a new anthology and wanted to include another story I had published in the *IT* days, a variation of the Faust myth called 'The Devil's Slander'. On offer was fifty pounds. I wrote back that this seemed a bit below the benchmark. By way of reply Simon Dwyer criticized my pretensions and said he would not be publishing my piece, adding that J.G. Ballard, Colin Wilson and, of course, Bill Burroughs had all fallen over themselves to accept the sum I had spurned. With my nose quite out of joint, I shared this news with Barry fully expecting him to come down on my side. This, after all, was the man who had reputedly priced work at his art-school shows in West End guineas when his peers were asking for shillings; this, the stickler for pecuniary recognition who had practically built the lucre-paved road that Damien Hirst and Tracey Emin were gleefully to waltz down. Instead, Barry was angry.

'They took your flag and stuck it in the map,' he hissed. 'Then you had to go and break the pole.'

# 2

AFTER THE incident with the commission, Barry and I continued to circle one another like two wary birds. I would come across him in M&M's, a bar near the new marina in Santa Eulalia run by two amiable Americans called Mario and Marty, who in terms of relative stature could plausibly be compared to Laurel and Hardy. Barry invariably drank scotch in a tall glass and would invite me to have the same, though usually I preferred a Spanish brandy such as Veterano. Then we would talk or rather I would listen.

This was not due to any desire on his part to dominate the conversation; it was more the fact he was speaking in a language I did not properly understand. The words were English but they were strung together in an odd order and peppered with old favourites such as 'homage' and 'civility'. His discourse was also sprinkled with allusions to things and people I was ignorant of, though this did not seem to bother him in the slightest. Added to this were speech patterns that ranged from a whisper to sharp stilted statements emitted in exaggerated barks. At times I felt like a student persevering with a demanding but fascinating lecturer. Even attempts to descend to a more pedestrian level by enquiring after his health or about the work being carried out on his house were countered by deeply arcane information concerning Buckminster Fuller or Alfred Munsell's system of categorizing colour, often conveyed with a half smile as though a confidence was being shared. Any effort, on the other hand, to join in the game and throw in a pun or surreal witticism, endeavours that a couple of Veteranos could only abet, invariably met with, 'Tip top this morning, thank you,' or a 'Must do something about the driveway.'

Barry seemed to spend a great deal of time in bars and there were several to choose from in Santa Eulalia: he was quite catholic in his tastes and might be found with a flute of champagne at Sandy's (a haunt of aristocrats and visiting actors, a little like an annexe of the Chelsea Arts Club) or swilling scotch with the steak-and-kidney pudding expats at the Harbour Bar. The heart of the town in those days, a heart that was to be surgically removed a few years later and with it a part of Santa Eulalia's charm, was the Kiosko. This, as the name suggests, was a kiosk-like building located at the top of the Paseo, which ran down to the promenade. The owner was a cigar-chomping man with a thick moustache and deep shadows under his eyes, who served the local absinthe and very large *sol y sombras* (sun and shade), a hellish mixture of anis and brandy. There were a few tables and chairs outside. There you would sometimes glimpse a gaunt man with the angular features of a bird reciting such gems as 'Ode to the Dutch Herring' to an appreciative circle of regulars. This was the poet Martin Watson Todd who became a close friend of Barry's. Martin loved Blake and Rumi but above all Diogenes, who ran through the streets of Athens one night, shining his torch into every face, desperate to find an honest man.

I had two incarnations on the island. The first was from 1976 to 1979 when I ran an international school in Santa Eulalia. In those days Martin and his wife Helga had an art gallery called Mensajero in the town. Martin's relationship with the gallery, however, as well as his marriage, came to an end. When I returned to the island in 1985, I spotted him in a bar foreigners seldom frequented. I went and joined him, a little shocked by the change in the prosperous figure I had known. He asked me if I was still writing. When I replied that I was, he said, 'You'll dry up.'

Ibiza studio
exterior c.1995

Yet there was warmth and wit in Martin especially when he was writing or reading out his poems. This made the loss of the notebooks that contained them, in the spring of 1988, a heavy blow. Martin kept these notebooks in a bamboo case, which was left in the boot of a hire car when it was returned to the airport. The car had been rented in Barry's name and the sculptor was mortified. The poet himself became increasingly reclusive, contracted tuberculosis and died in early February 1989. A year or so later the bamboo case turned up and Helga asked me to type out and edit the poems with a view to producing a book. I gave her a copy of the typescript and took one round to Barry.

The Flanagan house was about half a kilometre off the road between Santa Eulalia and San Carlos. It was a large, relatively new rectangular affair painted a shade of beige. In many ways it was a work in progress as extensions were added and alterations made almost continually throughout Barry's tenure. At one point he sold it only to buy it back a couple of years later. The new owner had the same first name as me and I was sometimes congratulated on my luck as people concluded, probably correctly, that Barry had only regained his property by paying a large premium.

There was a driveway to one side overlooked by the kitchen area on the ground floor, in which Barry installed a green Aga. Thick green carpeting then carried you to a large living area that took up most of the centre of the house. A stage-like platform to one side of this might at any one time support a cello, guitars, mannequins or armatures. A fireplace lay at the other end with a wall alongside that Barry used as a notebook, scribbling his thoughts in pencil on the flaky surface. Sometimes, when I visited, I would read any new jottings, which frequently acted as a barometer of his mood. Near this, French windows gave onto a garden that at that time was an untended expanse of weed and scrub. To the left of this was a work area consisting of a print room with etching and silkscreen materials, a kiln for ceramics, and a mould-making room shelved out with plaster, rubber, wax and scrim. Barry had everything he needed to make moulds and armatures, though any serious casting had to be done in London. Lying about outside would be armatures of prototype hares, ceramics and the triangular works he was making in mild steel. This area, like the house itself, was frequently in a terrible mess, strewn with wire, sand and various found objects that vied with each other to be integrated into a piece of sculpture. It was difficult to believe anything of form or beauty could emerge from there, though of course it did.

I gave Barry the typescript of Martin's poems and he began reading it, making appreciative little yelps as he did so. With no fire lit, the living area felt cold and a little damp, with wire and torn-up paper strewn across the floor and dust covering the sofa we sat on. After a while Barry led me into the room to the side of the living area, which was empty except for a woman's torso that had been cast in bronze and a small, round, almost featureless head with some wooden architectural blocks all jumbled together in no particular order. Barry tried different ways of assembling them, with my assistance, placing the blocks on their sides and then upright with the torso and head aligned in various positions. Finally an arrangement by which the blocks were placed in a row with the torso and head on top appeared to satisfy him. It gave the assembly an air of mystery or religion, like votive offerings for a rite. 'Tabernacle,' he said. The torso and head

OPPOSITE
Ibiza studio with component parts for *With the Head of the Goddess in my Hands*

with the blocks beneath them looked like something that would be carried so I proposed, 'Ark,' and then, 'Jubilee.'

As usual Barry did not seem to register the suggestions. We piled into the white Volkswagen van he was driving at that time and went to a bar on the San Carlos road. As we sipped our drinks, he took out his chequebook and fountain pen and I realized he was going to reward me for my editing work. He seemed confused by the amount so, having learnt from the commission incident not to look a gift horse in the mouth, I looked round to see if there was something in the bar that might provide a clue. The shelves behind the bar were lined with lighters. I suggested he count those. I do not think there were as many as a hundred but that was what he wrote, 'a hundred thousand pesetas', in brown ink adorned with the loops and elongated forms he favoured for the first letter of words. On the stub he wrote 'Richard communion Martin'.

Another friend of both Martin's and Barry's was a Dutchman called Leon Dupont. Leon was the former owner of a well-known bookshop on the Singel Canal in Amsterdam and decided to publish Martin's poems. They were printed in Amsterdam in the form of a small white A6 paperback. The cover bore a photo of a stone propped up in a field; this was the memorial Barry had made for Martin. The stone was thin and slab-like and had an oddly shaped triangular projection on its top left side. It bore a spiral at its centre, the symbol of Barry's hero, the eccentric French writer Alfred Jarry (1873-1907), around which Barry had carved the words 'the pleasance of the poet'. 'Pleasance' means a place laid out as a pleasure garden or promenade and is also an archaic form of 'pleasure'. The book appeared in March 1992. Poems from it were recited in memorial gatherings held for Martin on Ibiza and in London.

Barry produced a couple more stones with writing on them at this time. On one he carved the word 'Music', under this 'Pop' and under this 'Complaint', on the other 'Books Babble'. It was perhaps big headed but I could not help feeling there was a connection between these and my own activities, as when I was not deafening people on the guitar I was moaning about how little time I had to scribble.

Barry's reputation as a generous employer was growing: he needed housekeepers, cleaners, studio assistants, drivers and builders to maintain him, participate in the never-ending work on the house and assist with the art he was making. His resources seemed to be infinite and many local businesses thrived on generous orders for building materials, green carpeting, studio equipment, wood and wine. Ibiza, of course, had its fair share of the rich but most kept a slightly lower profile than Barry. Word went round that he had to spend the money or it would go on tax, and indeed he had had difficulties in this department in England. Speculation as to the exact size of his fortune fuelled many hours of conversation in bars and astronomical sums were frequently attributed to him.

Ibiza's expat community was divided between the haves and have-nots, the former being serviced by the latter. Those who transcended the provision of services, be it electrical, mechanical or housework, and became regular fixtures in the lives of their employers were known as handmaidens, a term applied equally to men and women. Barry was unusual, however, in the Pygmalion-like effect he had on people. At least two expat builders became working sculptors after a stint in his employ. Then there was Colin, the former cruise-ship crooner who went from being an electrician and odd-job man to editor of *The Artist*. Colin had been afflicted with Parkinson's disease at an unusually young age, and some felt this in part explained the sculptor's help.

Barry needed someone to handle communications for him so Colin managed these from a flat in Santa Eulalia. He was supplied with fax machines, the latest Macintosh computer, a scanner and state-of-the art printer. On this he began producing a newsletter: this took the form of a sheet of folded A3 on which he placed caricatures of leading lights of the expat community drawn by an American artist who normally offered such services to tourists in the Paseo, alongside reviews of exhibitions in local galleries, news of local events and editorials in which he gave his views on the arts and other matters. I contributed articles and poetry to *The Artist* and also to the rival that soon sprang up, called *The Argonaut*. The editor of the latter was a die-hard American hippie called Bobby Moustache, also known as Motor Mouth because of his ability to talk not just the hind legs but also the saddle and pack off a donkey. Typewritten and photocopied, *The Argonaut* was a more crude production than *The Artist*, but made up in sincerity what it lacked in glossiness. In the background to all this was a smiling Barry, a Midas, who if not exactly turning everything to gold brought zest to all the lives he touched.

Barry, of course, along with others at St Martin's College of Art, had produced his own magazine, *Silâns*, between 1964 and 1965, fifty copies of which were cyclostyled every other Monday morning and placed in Better Books to pick up for free, where they nestled alongside *The Marijuana Review* or *Fuck You: A Magazine of the Arts* (1962–65). Meanwhile in the basement, alongside the typewriter kept there for patrons to knock out a poem should they feel so inclined, Alexander Trocchi, writer and heroin proselytizer, would be stuffing books into his clothes, which he would sell later in order to finance his junk habit. Alternatively copies of Barry's magazine were given away at St Martin's, which was a few minutes' walk from Better Books on Charing Cross Road. *Silâns*, pronounced like the French for 'silence', included Barry's poetry of the time, as well as drawings. The magazine also published poems and articles by such contemporaries as Phillip King (Barry's allocated tutor at St Martin's) and extracts from writers such as Joyce and Tolstoy. *Silâns* bore witness to Barry's attempts to define his way as an artist, most notably in the supreme assertion of individuality contained in 'Letter to Mr Caro' (the sculptor Anthony Caro, also his teacher at St Martin's) which concludes: 'I might claim to be a sculptor and do everything else but sculpture. This is my dilemma.'

Several editions of *The Artist* had come out by the time its guns were spiked by the appearance of an anonymous and scurrilous parody called *The Electrician*, with an editorial commitment to 'demean and bemoan' and a leading article on forthcoming power cuts in Santa Eulalia. Notwithstanding this, I was a little envious of the editor and others on the payroll. I did not usually start teaching until late afternoon but even this seemed a gross incursion on the freedom to write I longed for. Moreover, though I mostly liked the children I taught I was incapable of disciplining them and more often than not the only weapon I had at my disposal, my belter of a voice, only served to make the cacophony louder. Barry would still often sidle up to me in bars but our conversations remained as convoluted as ever. At times we seemed to be discussing employment. I would prick up my ears and he would allude to bizarre-sounding tasks and errands but the words were in a code I could not crack. In the end, I did get

patronage, from a friend I knew from my first spell on the island. The first version of my four-hundred-page tome, set in the time of Nero, had attracted the attention of a London agent. As the bulk of the work focused on exile on Ibiza, and as I had told him I had transposed the present into the past, he suggested I do a rewrite with sections set on the island now. The conundrum was how to link the two. It was on the basis of this that my friend offered sponsorship. I was free at last to give up the day job and write.

The rewrite took just over a year. I sent it to London and after about six weeks heard from the agent. He did not like it. I had no work and could expect no more support from the patron. I did the only thing I could: I sat down and started another draft. I was doing a little private teaching but it was not enough, so one gloomy day in early 1992 I went to see Barry. The house was empty and seemed in a greater state of disorder than usual. I found him sitting on a sofa in the living area wearing a kimono and a morose expression; I heard later that the night before had been marked by heavy drinking and a fracas in a bar involving one of the town's leading dignitaries. Barry – who was fond of nautical references – said something to the effect that his mast was broken. In turn, I explained my predicament and must have made a reference to local beneficiaries of his largesse because he said, 'I don't look on you like the others.' By the side of the sofa was a shoebox, which he handed to me. On the lid, in handwriting more spindly than usual, he had written: *My concience* [*sic*] *knows the difference.* He told me to open the box. There were five of his pinch pots inside – small, round, hollowed-out examples of baked but untreated clay. 'Take these to the museum,' he said.

*Ubu sketch no.3: Pere Ubu*, 1974, Pen on paper, 5 ³/₄" x 3 ¹/₂" / 14.6cm x 8.9cm

# 3

I LEFT BARRY'S no wiser about my job prospects or the conundrum he had presented me with: which museum was I supposed to take the pinch pots to? There were two potential candidates. One was the Museum of Contemporary Art, located about midway up the little mountain by the sea known as Dalt Vila (literally 'Upper Town'), the old part of the city of Ibiza. It had been closed throughout the 1980s and had only just reopened, hosting an exhibition of work from the museum's own collection of artists based on Ibiza in the years 1900 to 1959 I had reviewed in my guise of art critic for *The Artist*.

The other possible home for the pinch pots was the Museum of Archeology, which was situated in the newer, flat part of the city called Eixample ('extension'). Sited next to the necropolis, a popular burial place in the ancient world due to the absence of snakes or venomous beasts on Ibiza, it had featured heavily in my research for my Roman book. Swayed by this and the primitive appearance of the pots, I phoned and arranged a meeting with the person in charge.

The director of the Museum of Archaeology had the sort of face you see often on the island, one in which the Phoenician lineage is still apparent. He greeted me amiably and sat facing me at his desk with an expectant look on his bearded features.

'A friend of mine thought you might be interested in these,' I said removing the lid from the shoebox, which I had placed on the desk.

He examined the pinch pots politely and at my urging removed one, testing the uneven, almost-brittle contours with his fingers. 'Where were they excavated?' he asked.

'A few hundred metres near the San Carlos Road,' I said. 'But they weren't exactly excavated.'

'Ah, they were found in a cave,' he said.

'Not exactly.'

'In a river bed?'

'Actually, someone made them.'

He nodded, seeming to find the information helpful, though it was of course blindingly obvious. 'Before the Romans?'

'A bit later, as it happens.'

'The Dark Ages?'

'Actually, my friend thought you might be interested. He made them. He's a sculptor called Barry Flanagan.'

No gleam of recognition dawned in the director's patient eyes. There was a chance, however, he knew Barry's work, not the early sacks and piles but the more celebrated hares. Unfortunately, I did not know the word for 'hare' in Spanish.

'His bronze rabbits are well known, though they're not really rabbits. They're bigger and have all sorts of ancient and magical associations. They box and go mad in March.'

'I'm not sure I can help you in this matter,' he sighed, pushing the shoebox towards me. 'Perhaps you should try the art museum.'

I did as he suggested but the way it came about had no connection with the shoebox. I was giving private English classes to the notary for Formentera, who lived with her husband, the chief vet on the island, in a beautiful finca near Santa Gertrudis. They were well connected and she mentioned one day that she was a good friend of Elena Ruiz Sastre, the director of the art museum. In turn I spoke of Barry and a couple of weeks later I found myself in Elena's office, a little witch's hat of a building clinging precariously to the city walls, with a splendid view of the market and warren of streets below. Elena was a young dark-haired woman from the mainland, who resembled Joan Baez during her time with Bob Dylan. She knew of Barry and asked me straight off if I thought he would consider staging an exhibition at the museum. She was so enthusiastic I did not tell her I thought it unlikely, given the sculptor's commitments elsewhere.

Most of us were swimming in a tiny pool whereas Barry was a very large fish regularly leaping off into the wide blue yonder. In that year alone, two giant hares had been placed on sixty-foot columns outside a hotel in Osaka, an event celebrated in an issue of *The Independent*, which also featured five smaller hares cavorting outside the *Economist* building on St James's Street in London. The sculptor had held a one-man exhibition in Tokyo and had been involved in group exhibitions in New York and Monte Carlo. If he wanted, it seemed, he could have his pick of the world's foremost metropolitan galleries and museums. Elena's request was a little like asking Al Pacino to appear in a student film project. Moreover, Barry's career was largely orchestrated by his London gallery and in particular by Leslie Waddington, the eponymous owner. I doubted if the latter would show much enthusiasm for so provincial a gig.

I mentioned none of this to Elena and promised I would pass on her enquiry. In turn, I had a question of my own. My parents had sent me a copy of *The Penguin Book of Spanish Verse* for my birthday. While browsing through it, I had come across a poem called 'Head of the Goddess in my Hands'. The verse was twenty-one lines in length and celebrated sculpture and the way art endures beyond life. I had enjoyed the poem for itself on first reading. Then I noticed the date beneath the title, 654 BC, which I knew was the date of the foundation of the city of Ibiza. The goddess of the title, I realized, had to be Tanit, the Phoenician moon deity who had been venerated on the island. The poem was by Antonio Colinas, a leading contemporary Spanish poet, who the blurb told me had received the King's Prize for Poetry. When I had mentioned my discovery to the notary, she told me Colinas was living on the island – she had met him and thought Elena knew him quite well. This proved to be the case, and Elena offered to contact Antonio and see if she could arrange a meeting.

I was excited by all this and went to see Barry the next day. I found him dressed in his usual kimono with sandals and thick green woollen socks. He seemed in a better mood than the last time and greeted me with the ritual query: 'Thirsty?' While he shuffled off to the kitchen for drinks, I noticed a couple of additions to the *pensées* pencilled above the fireplace. The first said:

> *Just because we're not at war doesn't mean we can all go around jumping into bed with one other.*

The next:

> *The hues of the ripple*

The second phrase sent me into a reverie. Barry's focus was not just the effects of an effect but the effects of those effects as well – a multi-dimensionality I detected throughout his work and in his attitude. Feeling like an eavesdropper, however, I said nothing when Barry returned with two long glasses generously filled with Bushmills and a miserly dash of water. He handed me one and then led me over to the wall between the living area and the kitchen. Near the light switch three birds were drawn in pencil: the highest one seemed to be singing while a lower one gazed up at him with an adoring look. This part of the work had a tender quality sometimes apparent in Barry's work, notably in *Molehill*, his drawing of two hares holding hands on the eponymous mound. Diagonally beneath the two birds was the head and upper torso of another bird who gazed ahead, apparently indifferent to the interaction of the others.

'We'll have to get this lot a job,' announced the sculptor, glancing at me with a gleam in his eye.

In turn, I had a couple of things to show him. The first was the shoebox, which I produced from the scuffed leather satchel I had adopted in preference to the ubiquitous Ibicenco baskets that tended to fall apart after a few months. I explained that my meeting at the archeological museum had not been fruitful; I had had more success, however, at the Museum of Contemporary Art. Barry told me to hang on to the pinch pots and listened while I related Elena's request. He was not as dismissive as I had supposed.

'As an independent artist I engaged with the steam and piston of commerce at the beginning of the 1980s,' he declared. 'Nevertheless, a sense of place requires location!'

Just as he had a holistic approach to materials, bending flax, hemp or cotton to unexpected sculptural ends in order to inhabit them, so Barry needed to embrace whatever place he happened

Detail of *With the Head of the Goddess in my Hands*, 1992, Gilded bronze and bronze on wooden blocks, 57 $^7/_8$" x 23 $^5/_8$" x 20 $^1/_2$" / 147cm x 60cm x 52cm

to be in: profoundly itinerant, he nevertheless liked his work to connect with wherever he found himself. I could see he liked the idea. Moreover, the recession that had begun in 1989 had dampened activity in London and elsewhere. He had, he added, been feeling a little fallow. He suggested I invite Elena to the house.

The second thing I produced was Colinas's poem. He asked me to read it to him:

> Dark clay shapes your face
> That careful time preserves.
> To be man or to be god is the same today:
> Only a little moistened earth
> Which an ancient sun hardened,

Mortal beauty, a very mature light.
But the time this fragile head has endured,
Which has contemplated for so many centuries
The death of others, which rests in my hands,
Has become fleetingly eternal.
On her brown face night falls,
Much sunset light falls on her two lips,
And one day more of our life falls.
It is a higher mystery, this of seeing
How her body accumulates centuries
While ours loses youth.
The mystery of two clays that have been born
From a single pit beneath a single fire.
But only to one of them
Did Art give the virtue of being divine
And, so, of never dying.

We sat in silence for some moments. Then he asked me to read it again. Barry's house was full of books and he was a subscriber to *The New York Review of Books* but I cannot recall one discussion with him that was intellectual for its own sake. He would happily let me babble on about writers, artists, history or some surprising new word origin I had come across, which occasionally he would employ, but his own ventures in such territory were oblique and cryptic to the point where I stupidly wondered if he had ever read a book from beginning to end. In turn, he would relate anecdotes about relatively well-known artists like Michael Craig-Martin or Gilbert & George, but never for the sake of name-dropping, of which he had a horror. As some of the names meant little to me at the time, I lacked context, and the stories flew by and that was it. Had I, however, researched matters and come up with an academic query about Anthony Caro at St Martin's in 1964, Barry, I am sure, would have immediately clammed up. 'I want art, without its myth, without its reputation[3],' as he put it. Despite fame, celebrity and the hares, which some saw as selling out, he stayed true to an attitude shaped by performance art, the Beats and most of all Alfred Jarry and his science of 'pataphysics, which Barry had come across when given in 1963 a special 1960 edition of the *Evergreen Review* devoted to the French writer.

OPPOSITE
*UBU production + pataphysical theme,* 1994, Blue pen and ink, ink-wash and correction fluid on paper, 11 1/8" x 33 7/8" / 28.3cm x 86cm

[3] Artist's statement, Rowan Gallery exhibition catalogue (1966)

PHYNANG
PHYNANCE

35 mm

Barry adopted the Jarry as his lifelong mentor, influenced not only by his writings but also by the woodcuts he made as stage designs for *Ubu Roi,* the Frenchman's famous play, which provoked a riot on its first and only performance as well as the ominous comment 'After us the savage God' from Yeats who was in the audience. This could manifest itself as allusion, such as Barry's deployment of Jarry-esque spirals or pear-shapes, or be more full on as in *Ubu of Arabia* (1976), a block of Hornton stone that almost by accident resembles a person, with a canvas hat wittily placed on the head. A later drawing, *Ubu Production + Pataphysical Theme* (1994), consists of sharply characterized figures in typical Jarry poses. This featured in a 1998 exhibition in France, Barry Flanagan and 'Pataphysics. The latter is Jarry's 'science of imaginary solutions', which investigates a realm beyond metaphysics inhabited by paradox and the absurd. 'Pataphysics is 'emblematic of the human imagination in revolt', as Barry put it[4], encapsulating both the system and its appeal to him. The motto of the College de 'Pataphysique, founded in Paris in 1948, 'I arise again the same though changed', more than gives the game away.

Jarry's impulse to turn every convention on its head led to him devouring meals backwards, beginning with the pudding and ending with peasant soup. He was a fanatical cyclist and often wore the appropriate gear but otherwise appeared in public in a stovepipe hat that was almost longer than his body, women's blouses, or a dirty white canvas suit and a makeshift paper shirt with a tie painted on it in India ink. Socially, he was popular but notorious for his bizarre staccato style of speaking, which placed equal stress on every syllable. The parallels with Barry are obvious – the singularities of habits, dress and speech. There may have been an element of conscious imitation in this on the sculptor's part, or more probably that he had by an act of willing osmosis absorbed Jarry into his being.

Another thing in common was a shared affection for alcohol, which Jarry called the 'essence of life', and my 'sacred herb'. When I first knew Barry, he was capable of drinking enormous quantities, sometimes more than a bottle of whisky a day. Alcohol was a means by which he attained certain states conducive to his work, 'the periodic dream' as Baudelaire described it, and enjoyed himself in the process. 'I'm a pissed artist,' Barry would say, 'not a piss artist.'

4 'Barry Flanagan in Conversation with Hans Ulrich Obrist', *Barry Flanagan Sculpture 1965-2005,* Irish Museum of Modern Art/Dublin City Gallery (The Hugh Lane Gallery: 2006) p.59

achras

Papa Durd

concience

3 packing cases

*UBU production + pataphysical theme,* 1994, Blue pen and ink, ink-wash and correction fluid on paper, 11 ¹/₈" x 33 ⁷/₈" / 28.3cm x 86cm

Jarry's life ran the classic bohemian course. He died in his dingy garret at the age of thirty-five of tuberculosis complicated or inspired by alcohol, malnutrition and vast quantities of ether. He was a prankster who mocked his own poverty, but he was poor and alone at the end, his last words being, 'Bring me a toothpick.' Barry, on the other hand, though immersed in the same tradition and partaking of the same ideas, turned his singularity to his advantage and became a very wealthy man. The extraordinary thing about this was the fact that the weapons he used, at least initially, were the same as Jarry's – transgressive notions with no obvious popular bite. Had Barry persevered with the conceptual work of his first period – the piles of blankets, the rope on the floor, *The stone that covered the hole in the road (the skull)* (1974), which appeared to be literally that (though Barry had in fact carved a landscape into the surface) – his fate might have been the same as the Frenchman's. Michael Compton, who curated Six at The Hayward in 1969, expected him to produce something 'paradoxically very cheap and yet unsaleable, a parable therefore of an ideal art'[5]. Aesthetically laudable as this may be, it sounds a sure recipe for starvation.

'There's no such thing as coincidence' was one of the few popular sayings Barry was happy to employ and it is a fact that in the late 1970s he attended business courses in top London hotels, sitting at the back, absorbing the terms and conditions he would present to the gallery. In cold commercial terms, the hare could be looked on as Barry's USP, yet from the early leaping ones through to *The Drummer* (1989-90), and *Nijinski Hare* (1989), this departure was as subversive and individual as anything else he did. Barry looked at the cliché of the tortured artist in his garret and found it a straitjacket. He believed people should be paid for what they did and deliberately took the romance out of his calling by describing himself as a tradesman and his practice as trade. In establishing that a living artist could command the same prices as a dead one and adopting a notion of authorship that could significantly boost production and so revenue, he paved the way for Britart. Ever the 'pataphysician, he achieved fame and fortune by first imagining the solution and then converting it into practice.

[5] Jo Melvin, ed., 'No Thing to Say', in *Barry Flanagan Early Works: 1965-1982* (Tate: London 2011) p.56

# 4

ON AN EXCEPTIONALLY warm spring day I met
Elena at the Royalty and we drove to Barry's house. Accompanying
us was a photographer, who was to take shots for the catalogue.
When we reached the house, Barry came out and greeted us in the
driveway. He was wearing his corduroy jacket, baggy trousers of
thick grey denim and a slightly grubby white shirt undone at the
collar from which dangled a striped tie. As he neared I noticed he
was limping and there was a red circle rimming the pupil of his right
eye and scratches running down his freckled cheeks.

Cupping his hands and moving them back and forth, Barry
ushered us into the house and led us into the living area. He pulled
the sofa towards the fireplace, invited the director and photographer
to sit, and then busied himself assembling a pyramid of twigs, small
branches and pinecones in the grate. Next he went to the table, tore
out a sheet from a sketchpad, fumbled in his pocket for a lighter,
found one and lit the paper, which he shoved between the kindling.
The wood was dry and a small curl of flame quickly turned into a
blaze. He then added a couple of logs of slow-burning olive, expertly

propping them against each other so the flames started to lick up at them. He straightened, turned with a satisfied air towards us, and wiped his hands together a couple of times. The cloudless day outside resembled a perfect English June, the temperature being somewhere around twenty-five degrees Celsius. It was soon much higher than that on the sofa but Elena and the photographer acted as though this was in the most perfect order and smiled up at Barry through the beads of perspiration streaming down their cheeks. For his part, the sculptor stood with one arm leaning on the mantelpiece lavishing a grin from his battered face on us all. Borrowing my adequate but far from comprehensive powers of translation, Elena expressed her delight to be in his house and broached the possibility of Barry holding an exhibition at the museum in August. A troubled look clouded the sculptor's face.

'All the stuff's in London,' he said, 'I've so little here: a few drawings, some family pieces, and bits in mild steel.'

'I will have everything you wish to display catalogued and insured,' she explained via me. 'In the catalogue there will be a few words from the president of the trustees, and I will of course write the introduction. After, I thought, a piece about you by a critic, a local one, but well-known and respected, might be appropriate.'

Barry beamed at her. Despite the sweat now coursing down her face, Elena beamed back: despite his limp, his damaged eye and dusty garments, she treated the man before her a little as if he possessed the trappings of a god.

'Might I in turn invite you to Rome this summer for Tony Caro's summer show?' said Barry. 'Richard, please translate.'

Barry's generosity often flabbergasted people and they thought he did not mean it. Of course, he always did. Elena looked a little flustered, briefly considered the logistics, and then smiled, which seemed to be a yes.

'Now let's have a look at the stuff,' suggested Barry.

Like Christian martyrs freed at the last minute from the stake, Elena and the photographer leapt to their feet and followed Barry to the table, where a folded sheet of A3 was hiding some work. Removing this, Barry began laying the drawings out. There was an exquisite series of moths and praying mantises he had drawn in Japan; a work called *Storyboard* (1984) consisting of six

OPPOSITE
*Alfred with Harlequin*
(also known as
*'little prince'*), 1986,
Blue pen on paper,
15 ¹/₈" x 11 ¹/₄" /
38.4cm x 28.6cm

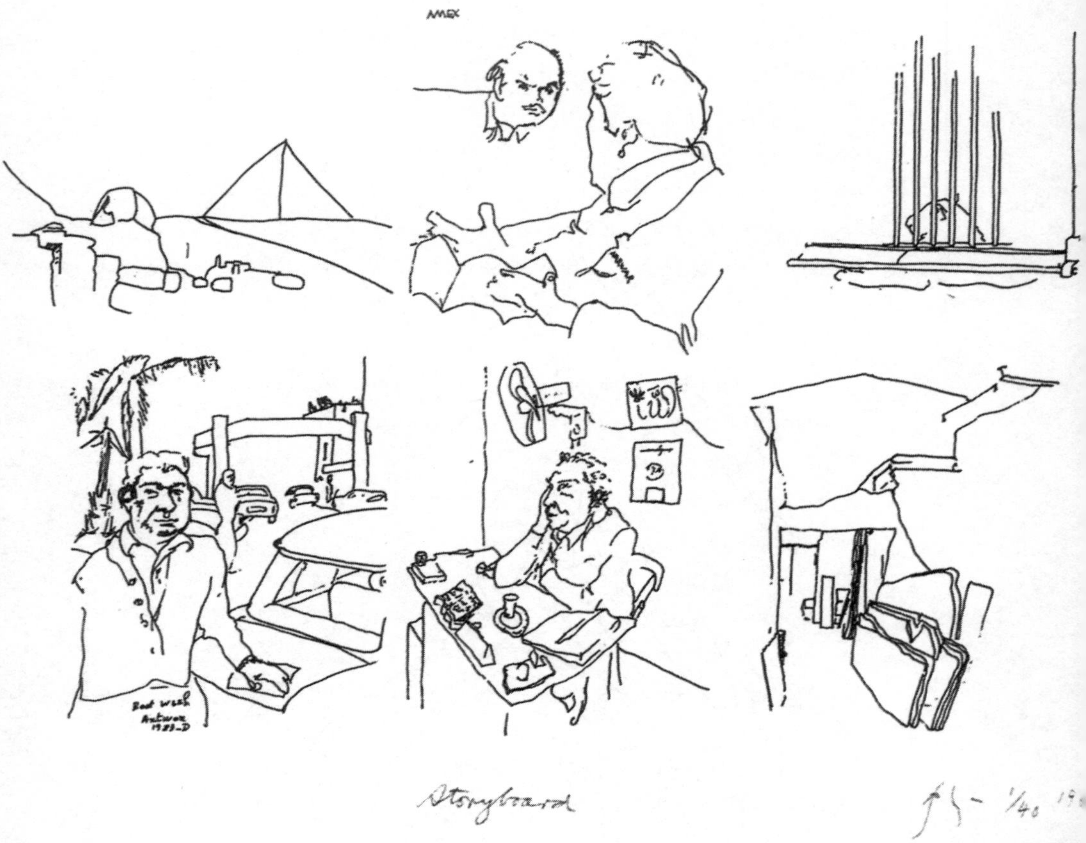


*Storyboard*, 1984

separate scenes depicting a visit he had made with Monica to Egypt; and *The Little Prince* (1986), a drawing of Alfred in his cradle with a jester-like doll standing over him. There were a few nudes in which one strong uninterrupted line in pencil exactly delineated the form. Then came *Parade* (1986) a sketch of a show at Sadler's Wells, and next a drawing of a woman looking at a picture with her back to the artist. This was called *The Curator* and could have depicted Elena, except it had been done in 1974.

'It is all a marvel,' the latter sighed.

The photographer started snapping and when he had finished we followed Barry to the platform on which there was a bizarre creature in bronze with the tail of a fish, two ears the size of table-tennis bats and a round smiling face with lines suggestive of sunrays carved beneath the eyes. This was called *Mexican Siren Restored* (1990), and as the last word suggests was, I believe, something Barry had 'found'. Behind this, leaning against the wall, was a cello with paper inscribed with Japanese symbols stuck to it. Barry had studied the instrument part-time at the Guildhall School of Music in 1964 and had gone on practising by the simple expedient of copying Pablo Casals' recordings. His fondness for the instrument is revealed to great effect in *Sixties Dish* (1972), a playful work consisting of a striped Parker-Knoll sofa with a cello on it pressed against a wall mirror in which the instrument is reflected.

We went into the garden, a mass of weeds sprinkled with garlic rose and mustard flowers. There was a mound of concrete in one part as though someone had started building a wall. Cables, wire, sacks of cement or sand were liberally strewn about the work area on the left where Barry had also installed a kiln. There was an armature of a hare and near this another man-size one in mild steel, which appeared to be running and seemed to hail from the more cartoon-like branch of the genre. Barry went up and patted it, dislodging some of the rust as he did so. On the long worktable that ran alongside the house there were some oddly shaped vessels formed of strips of clay with round orifices opening onto their dark interiors. Beside these was a small clay female form in which the breasts, belly and arms were bloated out of all proportion. This was *Bes* (1990), transmitted via Foxy.

*The curator*, 1974,
Ink on paper,
10 ¹/₄" x 8 ¹/₁₆" / 26cm
x 20.5cm

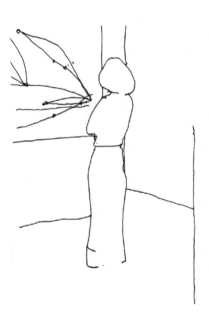

Anything Barry patted, the director rightly assumed was intended for the exhibition and she made little gurgling sounds of pleasure as the photographer snapped away.

'Thirsty?' Barry asked.

'Unfortunately, I have to leave now,' said Elena, 'but I cannot tell you how excited all this has made me.'

Smiling and affable, Barry escorted his guests to their car. We then went back into the house and had a drink. It had been thirsty work.

There was an unexpected sequel to this visit. Barry asked me to contact the photographer and bring him on his own to the house. I did this and a couple of days later I found myself standing at the door again with the photographer in tow and no one there to answer it. There was no car apart from mine in the driveway. I assumed Barry had forgotten our appointment. After the third knock I decided to give up and only as an afterthought pushed the door in a desultory way. It yielded and we entered to find a scene that evoked the *Mary Celeste*. There were cups half-filled with lukewarm coffee on the table in the reception area and the low murmur of a radio coming from the living area. I called out Barry's name but there was no reply: the house was definitely empty. I turned to the photographer and shrugged, wondering how I could excuse this. He was an affable man, however, and such a lapse of memory bore all the hallmarks of the eccentricity that was expected from the sculptor. Then the telephone rang. I went over and picked up the receiver. It was Barry.

'Kindly get on with it,' he said.

'I'm sorry, Barry, but with what exactly?'

He seemed surprised that I did not know.

'The birds, what else?' he demanded as though talking to a child. Then he put the phone down.

I hadn't a clue what he was talking about and thought of calling him back. The age of the mobile phone was not quite with us, however, and I knew from the background noises that he had been calling from a bar, but which bar I could not say.

There were birds in the garden of course: swallows, doves, and if you were very lucky the plumed hoopoe with its haunting cry and whirling wings of black and gold. Something told me this was not what Barry had meant. Then I remembered the birds on the wall in

*Bes*, 1990,
Bronze,
4" x 7 1/4" x 4 1/2" /
10.2cm x 18.4cm x
11.4cm

the living area. I led the photographer to them and he took several shots. A while later, Barry selected one of the snaps and it was made into an etching called *Passerines*, the name given to song or perching birds. An edition of eighty was printed plus twenty artist's proofs and their author would give me number two in March, 1994 – a month before I started another life.

On the way out I checked the wall beside the fireplace for any fresh musings. There were two. One said:

*It closed like an egg*

Beneath this was written:

*Is it my fault I chose life over employment?*

The second, I would learn later, was a riposte Barry had made to a belligerent tax inspector.

*Passerines*, 1994, Aquatint etching, 16 ¼" x 12 ½" / 41.2cm x 31.8cm

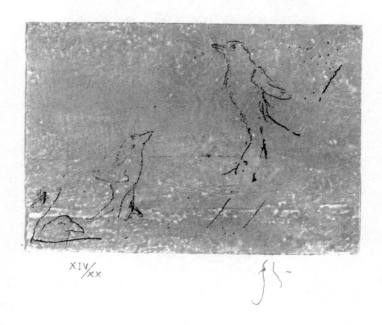

# 5

ON THE FOLLOWING Monday, Barry and I visited the museum. Originally built as the hall of arms for the Ibiza garrison in 1727, it is a long rectangular stone building with a V-shaped roof located on an outcrop of the bulwark of Saint John, one of many fortifications that attest to Dalt Vila's past as a citadel. The bulwark looks down on the food market, the Venetian-style façades of the old houses with their blues and ochre, and beyond them the harbour. We went through the high wooden doors at the entrance into the ground floor gallery, which was full of graphic work from the international print biennale. Elena was waiting with her assistant at the reception. She smiled but seemed nervous. She asked me to explain to Barry that because of the city council's sudden and unexpected decision to hold the next graphic show in October Barry's exhibition would have to be brought forward to June. This meant the catalogue would have to be completed in May if it were to be ready in time. I explained this to Barry, who had delegated all the initial spadework to me. The sculptor said he would give her an answer from London by the following Wednesday, but from his attitude, then and subsequently, I sensed his acquiescence.

After a quick tour of the posters and prints on display upstairs we descended the stone steps at the end of the gallery. These took us down to a large cellar with a semi-tubular roof and walls of old stone tinged with greenness. All that remained of mould that had been scrubbed away. This cooler place had two large bays, one of which we went to. It looked down on the cobbled way ascending from the market square, which disappeared into a gate flanked on either side by headless Roman statues, whose chipped togas Barry had admired on the way up. The cellar had been used originally as a storeroom for both gunpowder and arms as well as feed for the garrison's livestock.

'It makes me think of fires, of explosions,' Elena declared enthusiastically.

I looked at Barry, dressed as he had been for the last several days in corduroy jacket with baggy trousers, and wondered how he would respond to this intimation of a theme. He appeared not to have heard and was gazing fixedly at the chipped grey floor with that curiously absorbed expression, which I was to learn signified the combustion of an idea.

'We need a green carpet and the walls could do with a lick of paint,' Barry muttered.

Elena needed no assistance with translation.

'Carpet? Paint?' she repeated in alarm.

After its first decade of glory in the 1970s, the museum had spent much of the 1980s closed, a victim of budgetary restraints and political infighting. Elena had been appointed in 1990, but despite the success of the revived Biennale, Ibizagraphic 1992, and the show of work done by Ibiza-based artists I had reviewed, she was fighting an uphill battle over spending. She was both too direct and idealistic, lacking that cosy sycophancy that oiled the bureaucratic wheels. Moreover, as always, there was envy, in her case coming from the owners of the city's galleries. Her job was possibly on the line and a major exhibition by an artist of such international renown as Barry could only help to save it. Perhaps that exigent part of the sculptor that had been succoured by success was aware of this.

'A thick green carpet,' he repeated.

'There is so little time,' she murmured.

'I'd be at sixes and sevens without it!'

She made a note about the carpet in a little notebook, which

also included measurements for the framing of the drawings. Then she asked about invitations. This seemed to be a cue, for Barry extracted a roll of fax paper from the deep recesses of his inner pocket. The roll bore about six hundred or so neatly columned names and addresses, which commenced in Amsterdam and ended in Zurich. Dismay flickered across Elena's face as she read it, doubtless inspired by the inroads it would make into her budget: looked at another way, however, the sculptor had handed her a calling card to every major museum, gallery and dealer in the art world. One-way traffic was never Barry's thing.

'The journalist who is to write a piece in the catalogue is greatly looking forward to meeting you,' said Elena. 'As sadly we don't have as much time as we hoped, he was wondering if that might be possible this week.'

It was rare to hear Barry say 'Yes' or 'No'. He made the slightest inclination of the head – a semblance of a nod.

'You can meet him here, if you like. Shall we say Wednesday morning at ten?'

Another inclination.

'We live in a time of crisis for the arts,' Elena said. 'There is the general slump in the international market and the inability of new talent to display or market work. I believe, however, it is precisely under such conditions that true talent will thrive rather than in the spendthrift atmosphere of the last decade, which merely pampered the banal, the puerile, and the outrageous.'

Barry inclined his head again and then turned to me. 'Hungry?' he enquired.

Two events punctuated our exit. At the end of the narrow road that ran from the museum we came across a group of labourers working over a fenced-off hole in the road. Barry paused and observed their exertions with obvious relish. In 1961, while visiting his brother Mike in Montreal he had worked as a site hand and then with an Italian buggy gang, pouring concrete. I had also had a spell in the building trade as a maintenance carpenter but had a different take from Barry on the gross manipulation of matter. It fascinated him and he invariably became an observer when any building or road works were going on. A couple of the labourers noticed us, leaned on their shovels and peered back as though trying to make out if we were some strange new breed of voyeur. This seemed a signal to leave. As we did so, I glanced up and noticed a figure balanced on a pipe coming out from the stone wall. The figure seemed to be wrought in bronze and resembled nothing so much as a hare, a marching Flanagan one at that.

'Have you been up here without me?' I said accusingly, pointing up at the creature, which I was sure he had placed there by surreptitious means – liking to leave his mark on things, as he did.

'Very much not guilty,' he declared.

This was indeed true, though I would only find this out some time later when I discovered the hare had been there for many years, its origin and maker forgotten. Nevertheless, I still believed in omens and this one seemed propitious.

We went to Comidas San Juan, a cosy restaurant sited at that time on the second street parallel to the food market. Like its distinctive wall tiles, prices seemed to have remained unchanged since 1872, the year it opened – even in the early 1990s, when nothing seemed to cost very much, it was dirt cheap. It was a popular

venue and from two o'clock onwards you had to queue, resisting the temptation to glare at the relaxed diners savouring their pork chops or sole. It was still early, however, and we found a place to the left of the bar, a marble-topped table that evoked Montmartre, or for a reason I could not quite fathom, the pre-Civil War dictatorship of Primo de Rivera. Barry favoured nursery food and from the menu, which changed each day, he ordered chickpea soup to start with and fish stew for seconds. I chose paella and then lamb chops, which were stringy and came with butter beans and a solitary boiled potato sprinkled with parsley. A carafe of chilled white house wine as murky as piss was placed on the table along with a sliced baguette in a little basket and some very pale aioli on a saucer. We declined the olives.

Barry began talking about a theme for the show, and I realized Elena's reference to fires and explosions had indeed struck home, though not quite as she intended. The sculptor surprised me by referring to Elmyr de Hory, a brilliant forger who took refuge on Ibiza in the 1950s, and, protected by Franco, had churned out Rembrandts and Titians by the dozen, which were to embarrass many of the leading museums in the world when their provenance was eventually discovered. Orson Welles immortalized the forger in his film *Fake*. In the 1960s Ibiza was home to Clifford Irving, who, inspired by de Hory, had famously faked the autobiography of Howard Hughes. Banking on Hughes's notorious dislike of publicity, Irving thought he would get away with it but a single phone call from the Bahamas and a denunciation in the billionaire's reedy voice put paid to his scheme and landed him in prison. As far as fakery went there seemed to be something in the very air of the island that inspired such sleights of hand – an invitation to take the unreality one stage further and indulge in outright mimicry. More recently, in the pleasure palaces of Manumission or Pacha you could pretend to be anything you liked, and nobody would expose you or place any limits on your behaviour. Ibiza is the home of fantasy.

What Barry meant by 'fake', however, was of a more subtle order. He had made a hare called *Thinker on a Rock* (1997), and another named *Nijinski Hare* (1996). In both cases his source was clearly Rodin and had been acknowledged as such by the titles. The Venus of Willendorf had inspired *Bes*; yet this was not fakery, it was homage. There were found objects, such as the *Mexican Siren Restored*, which

you could argue was an impostor, but since the actual pneumatic drill Epstein incorporated into *The Rock Drill* (1913-15) or the urinal Duchamp signed as R. Mutt, a perfectly excusable one.

I suggested that archaeological references might supply a theme: the island's Phoenician heritage was there for the taking. Parody seemed too harsh a word but he had already done something like this with the drawings he had made of Etruscan sculptures in the museum at Cartona in 1974. With a sly look Barry told me these were the result of a snatched visit to Italy one Easter weekend. I thought of the academics who had written essays on Flanagan and the Etruscans. Donning the cloak of another epoch is fraught with hazard for a writer, so meticulous must his research and immersion in the period be. A painter or a sculptor, however, only has to borrow one emblem of a vanished culture to be pronounced an authority.

With fakery and parody dismissed, we were left with a prospect as blank as the marble surface of the table.

'What about a retrospective?' I suggested.

Barry flinched. 'That can wait till I'm dead. Besides, it's too impractical and costly to bring stuff down here.'

There remained the work in the studio – the sparse offerings of his sojourn on the island.

'It's all a bit light,' he muttered.

'You could make it darker,' I proposed.

'Very cute,' said Barry.

'Renate said she thought you should persevere with the pieces that exploited light.'

Barry did his little trick of not seeming to register statements that in fact had made an impact. He took out his Moleskine notebook and opened it at a fresh page. Then he rapidly sketched the mild steel piece in the garden, the one with the circle supporting a triangle. In the reddish-brown ink he used he added 'x 2'. Next he drew a pile of sacks and beneath them he wrote the phrase 'light on light'. I mentioned Bes and he wrote the word down. Then he added 'three pieces – Renate, Alfred, Annabelle'. I made a reference to ceramics and he said he could use a glass cabinet he had to display these. On the walls there would be what he again described as fakes, which I understood to mean drawings and hangings. Elena had requested the small bronze *Kouros Horse*[6] that Barry was in the process of donating to the town council of Santa Eulalia but as it turned out this would not prove possible.

The bill came and Barry paid. Conscious as always at such points of the discrepancy in our bank balances and embarrassed that it always seemed to be him who picked up the tab, I offered my share. Barry waved this away. 'It makes me feel grown up,' he said. With lunch we had drunk a litre of white wine, but as there was no coffee machine in the restaurant, probably because they could not afford to let their customers dawdle, we went to a bar on the waterfront.

OPPOSITE
Barry Flanagan with *Field Day 2* (known by Ibizans as *'Kore Horse'*), 1987, 60" x 72 ¹/₁₆" x 22 ¹/₈"

[6] *Field Day 1*, (1986). Sometimes referred to as *Kouros Horse*

It was a large smoky place with rickety tables occupied by old men in berets who chattered noisily in gruff tobacco-hoarsened voices as they played cards. Like Comidas San Juan it was a relic that had miraculously survived the incursion of lumpen tourism and the new standardized type of bar springing up everywhere, with clean white surfaces bathed in fluorescent light, wall-to-wall mirrors and an obligatory fridge with a glass door so you could be tempted by the ranks of bottled German fruit beers within.

Despite Barry's largesse as regards food and drink, my thoughts refused to budge from money. Was I not organizing an event that pampered to the almost baroque need to pay tribute to place I knew the sculptor possessed? This had involved meetings, numerous phone calls and the strain of interpreting his whims and indulging his caprices, never really sure if such terms were appropriate to an intelligence that used idiosyncrasy as a smokescreen. Now this very characteristic held my tongue, for if you asked Barry the time of day he would discuss Abstract Expressionism, mention Barbara Hepworth and he would say the weather was nice.

Barry's approach to being an employer was as multi-faceted and singular as his work. He had had his video fixed. Then, when it broke down again shortly afterwards, had reputedly sent fifty thousand pesetas to the man who had repaired it on the grounds that he needed further training. By contrast, he had devastated a studio assistant who thought he heard the sculptor say he would pay a phenomenal five hundred thousand a week and then found this was in fact fifty thousand. Still, two hundred thousand pesetas a month, which the fluctuations of the exchange rate apart could be loosely translated as a thousand pounds, was good at that time by anybody's standards and seemed to be the going rate for those in Flanagan's employ. What then should be the reward of the 'onlie begetter' of his next show, the 'spontaneous fixer' as he was to describe me, beavering away tirelessly behind the scenes for his greater glory? Was it best to broach the subject and name a price or should I wait for him to extend a generous hand in my direction of his own accord? I opted for the latter because I was entranced by this new world of museums and galleries, so different from being drained by a class of bolshie children. I was flattered by the reverence that stole across people's faces when they heard his name, thinking that some of the glitter might fall on me. It was fool's gold and shone all the more brightly for being so. I was hopelessly star struck, happy to wade through bogs and leap from ledges if I could call Barry Flanagan RA, OBE, my mate.

We drank espressos liberally laced with brandy, then switched to spirits, of which we had three or four. Then we had a couple more black coffees to sober us up for the journey back to Santa Eulalia. I drank a lot in Barry's company justifying this by the fairly dubious excuse that everything made more sense when I did so. I certainly felt more fluent in conversation after a few and better able to grasp the trapeze-like swings of his discourse – that at least is what I told myself.

*Trans fixed*, 1994

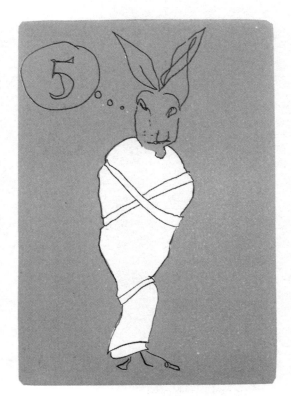

Les nouns de un leure en engleis

Þe mon þat þe hare i-met,
  Ne shal him neuere be þe bet,
Bote if he lei doun on londe
Þat he bereþ in his honde
  Be hit staf, be hit bowe,
And blesce him wiþ his helbowe,
And mid wel goed devosioun
He shal saien on oreisoun
  In þe worshipe of þe hare;
Þenne mai he wel fare:
'Þe hare, þe scotart,
Þe bigge, þe bouchart,
Þe scotewine, þe skikart,
Þe turpin, þe tiraet,
Þe wei-betere, þe ballart,
Þe go-bi-dich, þe sollart,
Þe wimount, þe babbart,
Þe stele-awai, þe momdart,
Þe euel-i-met, þe babbart,
Þe scot, þe deubert,
Þe gras-bitere, þe golbert,
Þe late-at-hom, þe swikebert,
Þe frendlese, þe wodecat,
Þe briodekere, þe brimbat,
Þe purblinde, þe fursecat,
Þe louting, þe westlokere,
Þe waldenye, þe sid-lokere,
And eke þe swikedere,
Þe stubbere, þe long-hroe,
Þe atauder, þe leiere,
Þe wilde der, þe leipere,
Þe shorte der, þe lorkere,
Þe winswolt, þe sculkere,
Þe hare-serd, þe hegerokere,
Þe dunfinge, þe deuhoppere,
Þe sittere, þe gras-hoppere,
Þe fitellist, þe folchittere,
Þe hert-list, þe ferurbinre,
Þe euerlhere, þe worteroppere,
Þe gobigrounde, þe sittesille,
Þe pintail, þe turne-to-hille;
Þe coue-arun,
Þe make-agrise,
Þe wite-wombe,
Þe go-mit-lombe,
Þe chousibe, þe choulart,
Þe chiche, þe couart,
Þe make-fare, þe breke-forewast,
Þe fnuattart, þe pollart,
His hei nome is ysewart;
Þe hert wiþ þe leperene hornes,
Þe der þa wonyþ in þe cornes,
Þe der þat alle men scornes,
Þe der þat no-mon ne-dar nemnem.
Wen þou hauest al þis i-said,
Þenne is þe hare misste alaid;
Þenne mirst þou wenden forþ,
Est and west and souþ and norþ,
Wedrewardes so mon wile—
Þe mon þat con ani skile.
Haue nou godnedai, sir hare!
God þe lete so wel fare,
Þat þou come to me ded,
Oþer in ciar, oþer in hred!

Amen


The Names of the Hare

The man the hare has met
  will never be the better of it
except he lay down on the land
what he carries in his hand—
  be it staff or be it bow—
and bless him with his elbow
and come out with this litany
with devotion and sincerity
  to speak the praises of the hare.
Then the man will better fare.

'The hare, call him scotart,
big-fellow, Bouchart,
the O'Hare, the jumper,
the rascal, the racer.
Beat-the-pad, white-face,
funk-the-ditch, shit-ass.

The wimount, the messer,
the skulker, the bleary-eyed,
the wall-eyed, the glance-aside
and also the hedge-springer.
The stubble-stag, the long lugs,
the stook-deer, the frisky legs,
the wild one, the skipper,
the hug-the-ground, the lurker,
the race-the-wind, the skiver,
the shag-the-hare, the hedge-squatter,
the dew-hammer, the dew-hopper,
the sit-tight, the grass-bounder,
the jig-foot, the earth-sitter,
the light-foot, the fern-sitter,
the kail-stag, the herb-cropper.
The creep-along, the sitter-still,
the pintail, the ring-the-hill,
the sudden start,
the shake-the-heart,
the belly-white,
the lambs in flight.
The gobshite, the gum-sucker,
the scare-the-man, the faith-breaker,
the snuff-the-ground, the baldy skull,
his chief name is scoundrel.
The stag sprouting a suede horn,
the creature living in the corn,
the creature bearing all men's scorn,
the creature no one dares to name.'

When you have got all this said
then the hare's strength has been laid.
Then you might go faring forth—
east and west and south and north,
wherever you incline to go—
but only if you're skilful too.
And now, Sir Hare, good day to you,
God guide you to a howe'ye-do
with me: come to me dead
in either onion broth or bread.

          from the Middle English

# 6

THE NEXT NIGHT I passed out on Barry's sofa at about four in the morning. Miraculously, he managed to make it to his own bed and even more remarkably responded to the alarm and woke me with strong black coffee at eight. Any enthusiasm we had for the bright fresh morning, however, had dissolved by the time we reached the museum where a jarringly cheerful Elena introduced us to a short, thickset man with a moustache. This was Mariano Planells, a journalist who contributed regularly to the island's main newspaper, the *Diario de Ibiza*. He had established his reputation in the 1960s with a series of books about Tanit and UFOs and the more mystical side of Ibiza.

'I am a grand admirer of your works, Señor Flanagan,' said Mariano.

'If I'd been a monk, I would have made a fine brew,' responded Barry.

Mariano tried to look like he had understood but his eyes widened in bewilderment.

The interview was to take place in Elena's office, the witch's hat balanced on the outer wall of the bulwark. Barry and the journalist

OPPOSITE
*The Names of the Hare*,
1982, Photographic
print, 19 $^5/_{16}$" x 14 $^3/_4$" /
49cm x 37.5cm

sat at opposite ends of a table, on which the latter had set up a cassette recorder. I assumed I was needed to glue together the cracks in Mariano's English as well as interpreting the Flanaganese. Barry was slouched on the chair looking as if he had spent the night in a hedge. His unshaven face had assumed a reptilian mode as it jutted upwards. There was a petulance that suggested it needed only a drop more of combative fuel to propel it to fury. 'Piss off!' he told me.

· About an hour and a half later Barry and the journalist emerged from the interview. I was standing outside smoking a cigarette and decided to ignore Barry as he wheeled past and disappeared into the recesses of the museum. Mariano staggered up to me like the survivor of an earthquake. A hangdog expression had replaced the confident air of only a short time before. In a voice that shook with bewilderment, he asked me if I was free to come to his office and make sense of the recording. The office lay about ten minutes away by car. Upon our arrival, with the air of a man handling a sacred icon, he placed the cassette in the recorder and pressed down the play button. At first there was only soft hissing and then a sort of rustling followed by a subdued moan. This was Barry, rasping and shrill at one moment, speaking in capital letters the next, and then fading away almost to a whisper:

'As my generation who were, we can safely conclude from the present yardstick, PUT UP TO IT!' [his bark provoked a high echoing whine on the tape] '… in the fifties …' [voice now soft and sibilant like a slowly unrolling wave] '… we were always … thirsty …' [a glass clinking against something as it was lifted from the table – sadly there was only water] '… I, Sir, am an ITINERANT, from one epoch to the next, from monk to painter in the court of a Renaissance Pope…' [the sound of the glass thudding down on the table].

Haunted by the excesses of the night before, Barry seemed to be thinking a great deal about the monastic life that day. Mariano reached forward and pressed the pause button.

'My English…' he said, not needing to complete a sentence, which, if it had had shoulders, would have shrugged.

'The problem isn't English, it is Flanaganese,' I said. 'Barry speaks in a sort of code and today he was being exceptionally cryptic. I doubt if even he could decipher this.'

'But what am I to do? I was going to use the interview as the basis for the piece but it's all like this. Listen!'

Things actually became more coherent as the session progressed. Barry spoke with enthusiasm of his Beat period and experiments with concrete poetry. He explained how he had begun another life in 1987, the year he had moved to Ibiza, but again emphasized his itinerant nature. He added: 'It is often said you cannot become a sculptor before your fortieth year, and in my case this is correct.' It did not seem to be enough to satisfy Mariano, however. He looked at me helplessly.

'I'll tell you what I can,' I said and began detailing what I knew of Barry's life before Ibiza.

Barry had been born in Prestatyn, a town in Flintshire, North Wales, on 11 January 1941. This would give rise to some confusion as at times he is described as a Welsh sculptor, at others, because of his surname, as an Irish one. In fact, Bill and Monica, his parents, had moved to Wales from Liverpool. Monica had run away from home to go on the stage and Bill had been a stage manager when they met; this, and his theatrical aunts and uncles in London, including Ella Retford, the musical star, and Bert, a high-wire artist, gave Barry an early affinity with the stage. 'The theatre is bronze,' he once said to me, which I took to mean that of all literary forms he considered drama supreme. While Barry was being educated at Catholic private schools (Foxhunt Manor prep school and Mayfield College) the family moved frequently – the root of the nomadic tendencies that were so much to the fore, at least when I first knew him, and which only began to wane in the new millennium.

His first art school was Birmingham College of Art and Crafts, where he began studying architecture at the age of sixteen, as well as modelling for and attending life-drawing classes. He changed to fine arts then 'bolted for' London after they tried to make him vice-president of the students' union. Over the next few years he held down a range of improbable jobs: doughnut-jammer, frame-gilder, chef, labourer, delivery van driver, and set-maker at Pinewood Studios for the Burton/Taylor epic *Cleopatra*. These were the day jobs that underwrote and informed his artistic development, itself bewilderingly eclectic, including cello classes, sculpture courses at St Martin's, and writing and performing concrete poetry. Indeed, Barry's original bent was more literary than visual, if a little unorthodox in nature. He succeeded, to his own satisfaction at least, in rhyming 'cider' with 'crazy' and delivered a silent lip poem at a poetry festival at Oxford University. He described himself at this time as 'the poet of the building site'.

One of Barry's teachers at St Martin's was John Latham, a tall, bird-like man with a shock of dark hair. Latham had been born in Northern Rhodesia (now Zambia) and as an officer in the Royal Navy witnessed both the sinking of the *Hood* and the *Bismarck*, with their terrible loss of life. After the Second World War he studied art and, perpetually on the lookout for a unified theory of everything, came to believe that time had replaced space as the primary issue in painting. Books were a frequent motif and he constructed towers, whose building blocks were encyclopaedias and art books, called *Skoobs* (books in reverse), which he would then set on fire. In 1966 he achieved notoriety by doing this to a piece called *The Laws of England* outside the British Museum, without notifying the police or fire brigade.

Barry found in John Latham a 'lateral thinker' like himself, and designed the invitation for an event called Still and Chew at Latham's home, during which the two artists and some students at St Martin's spent an entire night chewing a third of the pages of Clement Greenberg's *Art and Culture*, a recently published book that Latham had borrowed from the college library. Greenberg, an American, was an occasional lecturer at St Martin's and when there championed Antony Caro's rigid school of formalism. He believed, however, that the best avant-garde art was being created in the USA and Jackson Pollock to be its greatest exemplar, dismissing British art as 'too tasteful'. It was probably this remark that inspired the chew. The guests spat the result into a small glass flask, where it was submerged in sulphuric acid. Yeast was added and the mixture left to ferment. Nine months later the college library sent Latham an 'urgent' overdue notice. The artist placed the liquid in a glass vial, labelled it *The essence of Greenberg* and returned it to the library. Latham's part-time teaching appointment was not renewed. The Museum of Modern Art in New York later acquired the piece, now entitled *Art and Culture* (1966-9), consisting of the vial and various supplementary materials and documents.

While on nodding terms with the Arte Povera and Fluxus movements, Barry was a diehard maverick, his sails firmly set against whatever wind happened to be prevailing. The dominant orthodoxy at St Martin's, expounded by Anthony Caro, Phillip King and William Tucker, was for rigid structures in plastic or steel. Barry described such sculptors as 'girder-welders' and in complete contrast began working with soft materials like cloth, rope and sand, which took on different forms every time they were assembled. He counted himself fortunate, he told me, that his piles and heaps escaped the public outrage that greeted Carl Andre's *Equivalent VIII* (1966), 120 firebricks arranged in a rectangular formation, when the Tate purchased and exhibited it.

To mark himself out still further, the sculptor employed inscrutable titles like *4 casb 2 '67* (1967), a work consisting of four blue conical sacks filled with sand. The title is actually a matter-of-fact abbreviation of the materials employed and their date of use: four canvas sand bags number two 1967. Transformed by ellipsis the title takes on mystery, just as the materials themselves had been rendered into art. Jarry again was an influence when it came to the development of this system of annotation. In time, Barry's titles would evolve into pure poetry such as *Built Like a Tree, Flows Like a River* (1980) – strips of braided cloth, which, in homage to the two rivers that converge on Lyon, the Rhône and Saône, meandered across the floor of the contemporary art museum in that same city in 1980.

Barry's need to 'Engage with every possible means of expression'[7] synched perfectly with the frantic experimentation of the 1960s. He trawled through different media, producing films such as *a hole in the sea* (1969), shot on the beach at Scheveningen near The Hague – the use of a transparent cylinder created the illusion of the incoming waves disappearing into a giant hole. Other films included *Sand Girl* (1970), in which sand from a sack suspended from a ceiling poured and trickled onto a naked woman. For a brief period in the early 1970s he allied himself with the Artist Placement Group, which sought to attach artists to industries with a view to using the materials at hand. His subsequent resignation may have been inspired by the realization that rather than attach oneself to industry it was better to become one. Through the rest of the 1970s he marched to the beat of his own eclectic drum, exploring ceramics, furniture design, dance and choreography.

In the closing years of the decade, however, Barry's approach subtly altered. There was deliberation in this, as his attendance at

[7] 'Submissions on an Application to RCA'. *Silâns*, Issue 6 (January 1965)

business courses attests. He had become increasingly resentful of 'the dreadful way in which money punishes art' and had at one point resorted to printing his own 'funds' in denominations of five, ten and fifty. Each note was marked, and thus authenticated, by the artist's blue thumbprint. The notes were offered in exchange for help or materials. (Any lucky takers will find that one Flanagan note is worth many times its face value today.) The 'funds', however, did not cover the needs of his family – a wife and two growing daughters – nor did the odd jobbing he was still forced to do. The shows he put on at the Rowan Gallery for the best part of a decade helped shore up his reputation but made little difference to his pocket. Increasingly focused on the notion of trade and acquiring the means to pursue this, he found an ally in Leslie Waddington, joining the latter's gallery in 1976.

It was not until 1979, however, that he began to make the marvellous hares with their wittily human characteristics. Interest in the animal had been a subtext in the cultural manifestos of that decade. *The Leaping Hare* by George Ewart Evans and David Thomson came out in 1972. Drawing on countrymen's talk, science, literature, mythology and superstition the authors produced a comprehensive compendium of hare-related lore, locating the creature in history, mythology, poetry and art as well as nature: the hare was chimerical and mysterious, intimately associated with the moon, fire, and surprisingly airports; the hare was a witch and a trickster capable of all sorts of magical acts, including vanishing; the hare's heart was very large, weighing from 1 to 1.8 per cent of the total body weight of the animal (in rabbits the heart weighed only about 0.3 per cent of the body weight). This will come as no revelation to the numerous beneficiaries of Barry's generosity over the years. Leslie Waddington relates how the artist instructed him to give the proceeds of a prize worth many thousands of pounds to a young French sculptor: an act, he describes, with a tone of wonderment in his voice, of almost supernatural generosity, which you could not expect from any another artist or indeed human being.

In 1979 Kit Williams brought out *Masquerade*, a children's book that focused on the quest for a golden hare. To go with the book, Williams crafted a hare from eighteen-carat gold and jewels, in the form of a large filigree pendant on a segmented chain. He sealed the hare inside a ceramic hare-shaped casket in order to protect it from the soil and foil any attempts to locate the prize with a metal detector. The book sold in the hundreds of thousands and the obsessive quest for the hare became a worldwide sensation. Williams had put the hare on the map, both literally and metaphorically.

Barry himself was inspired to use the hare after seeing one bounding across the Sussex Downs. According to Henry Abercrombie, more usually known as 'Ab', (the boss of what was then A & A Sculpture Casting Ltd), the sculptor then bought a dead one from Cramer's, the Camden Town butcher, and took it to the foundry. He twisted the animal's legs to make it look as though it were leaping and used it as a reference point for a clay model, which he gave to the foundry to mould and cast. That characteristics of the animal tallied with the whimsical and unpredictable side of Barry's own nature was a bonus – he had, after all, long styled himself as British sculpture's lord of misrule.

In one bound, the sculptor had leapt into figurative work and had done so in bronze, a material his contemporaries largely considered obsolete, rendered so by the dead weight of tradition. It had also been unfeasible for Barry to do this before because of cost. 'If you want to make the cast from a modelled piece more permanent, bronze is the thing,' he said (ironical if you consider the vogue for Auto-Destructive Art in his youth). This quest for permanence could also be traced back to the fate of earlier sculptures, such as one at Laundress Green, Cambridge in 1972, four upright resin and fibreglass columns resembling totem poles. The sculpture was abused by critics and then by students who attached washing lines and hung clothes from it before removing it completely. Barry's response was sheer poetry: '...the storm came later, before the light of summer had a chance to play on the surfaces of shape, to dry to a husk the sadness of a hard winter.' Such vandalism propelled a need for more durable materials that took him to Pietrasanta in Italy in 1973 to learn stone carving. Bronze was a very logical stop on this route.

The hares brought Barry fame and riches. In 1982 Lord Snowdon photographed him for *Vogue*. He sits on a chair in an artist's smock, alongside a large leaping hare on the floor, his face turned to the camera, his hair unruly. In the same year he represented Britain at the Venice Biennale. Money brought power and independence but was not the only result of leaving the garret. Maverick and obscure artists are often doomed to solitary – think Blake, think Jarry – and Barry was no longer alone but slotted into the scheme of things. There was the foundry, the gallery, the media, and important collaborations such as the one undertaken in 1983 with Seamus Heaney: *The Names of the Hare* (1982), a translation of the medieval poem produced in a broadsheet and adorned by Barry with three golden leaping hares. The poem contains a long list of names that the hunter can use to ward off the devilish creature: 'the hug-the-ground, the lurker, the race-the-wind, the skiver'. As time went on Barry may have felt typecast by his creation and the commercial pressures that success exerted on his practice. Nonetheless, it had carried him like a tsunami to where he was today, buoyed by or beached upon Ibiza, depending how you looked at things.

# 7

WHEN THE CATALOGUE for the Ibiza exhibition appeared, its cover was equally divided between gold for Barry and silver for Marcel Floris, the French sculptor who was to share the show. The texts were in Catalan, Spanish and English, but the poor translation of Planells' text made for observations such as, 'His geometry implies the service of perspicaciousness.' When I asked Barry what he thought of the text he replied, 'It was already finished before we met. He wrote about himself, not me.'

The sculptor went on to describe the Ibiza exhibition as the most important he had ever undertaken. This surprised me, as it was a relatively provincial affair and not even a one-man show: but Barry had never before exhibited in his own backyard, and as the costs and red tape involved in transporting the famous hares to Ibiza was prohibitive, the result was inevitably a more personal show. (The heads of his children, the pieces from his own collection – some dating back to his teens – and most of all *Head of the Goddess* (1992), where Annabelle gazes up at the belly of her mother, was work of a more private nature than he was used to showing.) It had also been a long time since he had so actively participated in a hang: others largely did the donkey work, as was the case in a forthcoming show he was having in Paris. Inadvertently, I had dragged Barry back to his student days – he felt like a novice who had to prove himself again.

The exhibition was to open on Friday, 5 June, so commencing on the Monday of that first week of the month we had five working days for the hang. 'I am a 'pataphysician,' Barry had announced to Elena and things did get off to a suitably absurd start when he embarked on a convoluted discussion with the three workmen from the town hall who had been detailed to collect the sculptors' pieces. Only when we ran into the director, fuming in her car after a two-hour wait, did the truth emerge. The men had been detailed to collect the work of Floris. This event put paid to any hope of work that day, and we retired to the bar in order to explore the implications of Jarry's dictum that it is 'the use, and even more the abuse, of fermented liquor that distinguishes men from beasts.'

On the Tuesday I managed to get Barry to the museum at half past ten for a press conference at twelve thirty, temporarily relieving the fraying nerves of Elena and her staff. In the right-hand gallery we were greeted by the order and precision of Floris's platinum mobiles, which had been assembled with military exactitude the previous

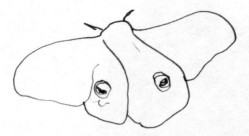

*Japanese Moth*, 1983, Pen on paper, 11" x 14 15/16" / 29.7cm x 37.9cm

afternoon we had spent in the bar. In the left-hand gallery, cluttering up the floor, were piles of Barry's drawings, sackcloth hangings and sculptures. In their midst, a large, abstract, metal sculpture did its best to fade into the background, like an unwelcome guest at a party. This was a piece Barry had decided to omit from the show – the workmen, eager to make amends for the previous day's run-around, had brought it anyway. After arranging for its expulsion Barry set to work.

It was like watching an arrow that had wavered and zigzagged and even rounded a tree suddenly hit the bull's eye. There was a rapt expression on his face as he hung drawings in one of the twin bays that overlooked the Gate of the Sea. 'More has happened to less,' he had commented earlier. Of the forty drawings that had been framed he eventually used just under half, selecting sketches of models, friends and family as well as those of moths and praying mantises, the latter the fruit of one night in Japan in 1985. In places the walls were very hard and the nails bounced out, one nearly taking out my eye.

Next he turned his attention to the gallery's far side wall where he placed six cloth hangings he had made in the 1970s. The cloths hung from bamboo poles and were daubed with various designs: two eights in *Double Eights* (1976); a white circle on a square red and brown background in *And Then Among Celts* (1977), and, in the case of *Celebration* (1973), a large penis with balls against a red background. Some time before Barry had said to me 'Think how, what, why and

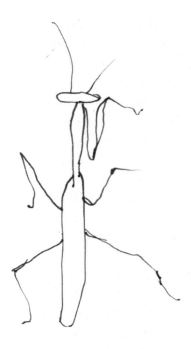

*Insects 7*, 1987,
Etching on paper,
4 ¹¹/₁₆" x 6 ⁹/₁₆" /
11.9cm x 16.6cm

when,' and I realized he had posed himself these same questions, as to how to fill this half-domed gallery that had once housed the arsenal and cattle of the city garrison.

Two identical rusty pieces in mild steel were to act as a centre-piece for each bay. Together they shared the title *Homage to Miró* (1988), and each consisted of a triangle supported by a circle. Cut out in the triangle was the shape of a crescent, and beneath this two linked wings and then a large circle. The design had been deployed by Jarry in his woodcuts and then borrowed in tribute by Miró. The pieces stood on three right-angled propeller-like legs, which sloped out before meeting the floor. To alleviate their sharpness Elena had suggested ringing the pieces with sand. 'Salt,' Barry now suddenly declared, and the decision was perfect, for salt and rust harmonize in nature as much as branch and leaf.

Then, to my amazement, Barry announced his intention of using the poem to which I had introduced him, 'Head of the Goddess in my Hands'. Thanks to Elena I had spent a pleasant afternoon with the poem's author, Antonio Colinas, in the gated urbanization he lived in a few kilometres from Ibiza town. Colinas – an avuncular man with a moustache and a distinct aura of self-possession – and I had discussed poetry, he giving me his latest work *El Silencio del Fuego* (The Silence of Fire), and I reciprocating with some of mine in the more humble form of a leaflet I had made from folded sheets of A4. This, in tune with where I was living, was called *The Blue Nest* and bore on its cover an engraving of the creek by my friend Bill Fulljames, an English artist living on Ibiza.

Barry had finally solved the riddle he had been wrestling with, that of the torso, the small head and the architectural blocks. He stacked the last so as to form a rectangle, placed the newly gilded torso on these, and then positioned the almost featureless black head as though it were gazing up at the belly. His idea was to rest the head on a photocopy of the poem and he asked me to bring one with me next time. This seemed to me 'the hues of the ripple' in action, a matrix in which poem and sculpture amplified a common theme to create a unique marriage between genres. It was also a further example, if any were needed, of the way a suggestion would percolate through Barry for a while and suddenly emerge distilled into a new and stronger form. The torso, incidentally, had been modelled on Renate using a shop-window dummy as the armature. Bill Fulljames had done the casting at his studio in Santa Gertrudis. During this one of the nipples had accidentally broken off, much to Barry's fury. The nipple had been replaced.

Having set up the sculpture, it was time for the press conference and we joined Elena and three local journalists. Also present was a tall lanky man with thick white hair and beard. This was Marcel Floris, who was then in his late seventies. In fact the poster for the exhibition, examples of which were hanging at various points in the room, bore the numbers 41 and 14 against a gold and silver background respectively. 1914 was the year of Floris's birth, and 1941 was Barry's. This sort of coincidence is called *una capucha* in Spanish, Elena informed us.

Dressed in a dark green Armani suit and a striped tie, Barry was more presentable than usual, and when it was his turn to be interviewed, responded on a much more even keel than he had with Planells. Despite this, called upon to translate simultaneously,

I found that what he was saying punished my dubious linguistic gifts as he vaunted the Celts and his intense relationship with the materials he used, describing clay, flax and hemp almost as living things with distinct personalities. I hadn't a clue how to translate 'flax' and for 'hemp' said 'hierba', which meant 'grass' and made the journalists chuckle. According to the next day's *Diario de Ibiza*, Barry expressed a preoccupation with 'the feminine principle that is present in all culture' and when speaking of *Head of the Goddess* mentioned 'the prevalence of a goddess on Ibiza, the Punic deity Tanit, who presided over culture on the island in antiquity.'

No more work was done that day or indeed on the following morning. We had an arrangement to meet at M&M's but though the agreed time was ten there was no sign of Barry until eleven. In the meantime, sitting at a high stool by the plate-glass window, I had time for two coffees served in a glass, a croissant halved down the middle and toasted, and more untipped Camels than I care to recall. During this, the regulars trickled in like workers clocking on for a shift, until the sunny terrace was filled with shady faces. A few minutes before eleven, I went to the phone booth by the toilets and called Elena. She sounded worried: everything was in place to proceed with the hang, but where was Barry? I did my best to reassure her, pointing out that the sculptor's relationship with serial time was unorthodox but that he always delivered.

Barry appeared about ten minutes later, shuffling along the terrace with that peculiar gait of his in which the upper part of his torso was pushed forward as if trying to catch up with his upturned face. His hands were thrust into his pockets except for his thumbs, which clenched his jacket from the outside. It was interesting to note the effect his appearance had on the regulars. Eyes glassy with hangover suddenly glistened; mouths which had had nothing to say rehearsed their best lines. Perhaps something similar occurs in ant nests when the queen appears, for this dishevelled man, his hair uncombed, his collar askew, who resembled the owner of a rundown bookshop, seemed like King Midas and Father Christmas rolled into one. Greetings rang out on all side, which the great man (I was glad to see) affably returned. He joined me at the bar and ordered a whisky for himself and a *carajillo* for me.

'Different time zone,' he said, nodding in the direction of the distant hills where his studio lay.

The bar, I noticed, was slowly filling up with women in jumble-sale garments who began to circle him from behind in a predatory manner. A short woman with a querulous face and spiky straw-like hair, which she obviously cut herself, darted from the pack and positioned herself to one side of him.

'I have to see you,' she said in a fluted kind of English whose minor notes were composed of French vowels.

'I am all before you,' said Barry, lavishing a smile on her.

'I mean we must talk. I have something very important, a show in Ibiza next month, but I need thirty thousand francs to import my big pieces from France.'

'And the small ones?' asked Barry quite unruffled by her demands.

'Why, they're here.' She seemed surprised.

'You see,' he said.

'See what?'

'Less is always more,' he took a large gulp of his J&B, 'but I, Madame, am always being asked for *more* of *less*, being more or less a BEN-E-FACTOR!'

Shifting his body he faced the bar, his face tilted petulantly up, and clinked his glass against the shiny metal surface. Mario, the sardonic barman from Chicago who suffered in his private life as well as from several of his regulars, glided over and refilled Barry's glass. The barman glanced at the woman and then frowned at Barry as if to say, you've got another one on your back. Barry tapped his tubular glass at a point somewhat higher than that to where Mario had filled it.

'More,' he said.

'Less,' I could not help counselling.

Mario frowned at me with one eyebrow raised. Now I was the monkey on the great man's back.

There was nothing else for it. 'The museum… ' I began.

'What a wonderful place,' sighed Barry, 'and Elena, how kind, how accommodating, what wisdom resides in that young eye!'

'We have to go there.'

'EVERYONE SHOULD GO THERE!' Barry declaimed, rocking precariously on his stool as, with a wide sweep of his arm, he took in not only those in the bar but the denizens of the terrace as well. 'This lot should be FROGMARCHED up that hill and be forced to KNEEL before her.'

Mario was washing glasses as though nothing out of the ordinary was taking place. The French sculptress with her oddly childlike face remained glued to our side.

'You will have it all back, you will see,' she announced breathlessly. 'It will be a huge success. I must see you.'

'Here I am.'

'At the studio, I mean. Can I come today?'

Barry made the slightest inclination of his head and smiled.

'In two hours?' Her glee was childish.

The sculptor retained the same imperturbable smile.

'We have an appointment,' I hissed as the sculptress drifted out of earshot.

'Why wasn't I told?' Barry hurriedly gulped down the last of his whisky and rose from the stool. Feeling like a skipper on the bridge of a storm-tossed vessel, I steered him out of the bar. On the terrace, though, he was hailed by some new arrivals and holding his arms straight out in front of him as though being arrested he scurried over to their table and collapsed onto the chair that was immediately made available. I glanced at my watch. It was a quarter past twelve. There was nothing else for it but to return to the phone booth and call Elena.

'But everyone is here,' her tone was agitated. 'There are so few days left.'

I did my best to reassure her, but what could I say? Barry was as unpredictable as the wind.

'Tell him we have the salt,' she signed off in the plaintive tones of a siren reduced to her last song.

On returning to the terrace I saw to my dismay that Barry had a fresh glass before him and was definitely becoming frisky. Every chair around the table was filled and those with him bore the familiar look inspired by his company, at once admiring and bewildered. I went over, leant down and whispered in his ear.

'They have the SALT,' Barry repeated to the entire company as though they would share the joy that flushed his features. None of them, of course, had the slightest idea of what he was going on about.

'Did they get the pepper?' asked a wag.

Disguising my annoyance, I straightened and returned to the bar where Barry joined me about two plain Camels later.

'Thirsty?' he asked.

It was pointless pretending I wasn't and two drinks quickly appeared, served by the unflappable Mario.

'Anything on today?' Barry asked.

'We're supposed to go to the museum.'

'Did they get the salt?'

I nodded.

'That's good, that's good,' Barry repeated, rocking back and forth on his heels. 'Then we should go.'

The moment we were outside, however, Barry made a beeline for another table and cheerfully joined the occupants. A dreadful thought occurred to me. I remembered how the poet Swinburne was nursed through his alcoholic delirium by the lawyer and minor writer Theodore Watts-Dunton, and wondered if I was on the way to becoming that ultimate handmaiden's heir. In fact, as things turned out, if anyone was to play the role of Watts-Dunton, it was Barry to my mad poet.

# 8

A SCHOOL OF THOUGHT existed that to render Flanagan into another language it was first necessary to translate him into English: there was an oracular quality to his pronouncements that could leave the listener with a sort of vertigo. At the same time, his manner of speech possessed an originality as compelling as that he applied to canvas, sand or bronze. To back away, dismissing what he said as eccentric nonsense, was to be duped by a smokescreen: the madness in the method. This applied equally to what he did. I often felt I was peering at a distant wood while he was sauntering amongst the trees admiring the patterns on the barks.

In the end on that Tuesday we did not go to the museum at all but had an M&M brunch of eggs, sausages, beans, grilled tomatoes and toast. Then we went in my old Dyane 6 out to San Carlos and visited a supplier of feed for cattle and pigs. We found him outside his barn loading sacks onto a truck. The sacks were filled with carob beans, which the Dutch called Jacob's bread and are used as food in wartime. The supplier was a lanky man with a thick black moustache, beetling eyebrows and bloodshot eyes. I said we had heard he might have some sacks for sale.

'That would depend how many you want and when for,' he said.

'About thirty for tomorrow,' I replied.

'I can give you fifteen of these,' he indicated the sacks he was currently loading by kicking one. They were made of thick brown hessian and had the name of his business faintly printed on them. 'The other fifteen I've got in the barn.'

'Are they a different type?'

'Yes, but what does it matter? The feed's the same.'

'Actually, it's the sacks we want.'

He shrugged. It made no odds to him. I explained the situation to Barry who told me he would like to see the other sacks. The supplier led us into the barn. There was a heap of light-coloured sacks to the left, which were made of flax. The supplier slapped one. Barry approached, felt the material with a sort of reverence and then nodded.

'Fifteen of each then,' I said. 'Can you bring them to the Museum of Contemporary Art in Dalt Vila?'

'Are they keeping pigs these days?'

'There's a lower entrance at the back. You should park there. The sacks are to go into the basement. They'll only be needed until the end of the month, then you can collect them.'

'I don't do sale or return,' he said. 'What's sold is sold.'

It was at this point Barry decided to join in the conversation. '*Por favor*,' he said, adding an extra syllable at the end that sounded like '*rey*', the Spanish word for 'king'.

'You'll get the normal price,' I said. 'It's just we only need them for about three weeks. So if you want to take them back you can.'

Far from allaying the supplier's doubt my reassurances only seemed to be heightening his suspicion: 'What do you want them for?'

'My friend is an artist. He's going to exhibit them in a show.'

'Sah, this son-of-a-bitch world is getting madder than ever!'

'*Por favor-rey*,' said Barry.

'I'm not your fucking king!' the supplier responded.

The fields of the Morna Valley were so golden and immaculate as we drove back in the afternoon sun that it was as though we were on another planet: a frequent feeling on Ibiza and one that was sometimes true. Just off the road after the bridge we stopped at Can Correu, Barry's local bar. The curly-haired owner, who I had seen grow from skinny boy to thickset man, barked 'Please! Thank you very much!' in

*light on light on sacks*, 1969, Hessian sacking and projected light, 84" x 108" x 84" / 213cm x 274cm x 213.4cm at '6 at the Hayward', Hayward Gallery, 1969

English and shook our hands warmly. He had told us where to get the sacks and was pleased we had clinched the deal. Such success demanded celebration and he poured Barry a J & B and me a Veterano. Obviously the day's real business was concluded and we were free to join Jarry in his contempt for the 'victims of that poison, water, so powerful a solvent and a corrosive that, of all possible substances, it has been chosen for the washing of our bodies and our clothes.'

: : : : : : : : : : : : : : :

When we arrived at the museum on the Thursday morning, the huge oaken doors in the basement had been opened to reveal a cobbled courtyard, in which stood a truck. The supplier from San Carlos was unloading sacks from this, which, assisted by a teenage boy, he carried into the gallery and stacked in a pyramid-shaped heap in one corner. A smell began teasing our nostrils, the rich earthy pungency of sacking, which had not been there since the garrison. Barry had ignored the gunpowder but gone for the livestock, or at least its feed, big time, I reflected. Halfway up the opposite wall a shelf had been erected on which we placed a projector. When Barry had first assembled *light on light on sacks* at the Hayward Gallery in 1969, the beam cast by the modified lens framed a rectangle of light on the sacks themselves. In Ibiza, the beam hovered above the heap.[8]

When Barry was satisfied, we went over to the bay where two large sacks were leaning against the wall. The sacks were filled with large crystals of sea salt collected from Salinas, where the salt flats have been in use since Roman times. We emptied one sack around the first *Homage* and the other round the second in its separate bay. As Barry must have visualized, the combination of shiny crystals and rusty mild steel induced a synergy that was stunning.

At this point we were interrupted by Elena and Antonio Colinas. Elena introduced the poet to Barry and we all went over to the golden torso on its rectangular base. The small black head gazing up at the torso was now resting on a photocopy of Colinas's poem. Far from looking pleased, the poet seemed quite put out.

'If you use a photocopy, the exhibition will be a disaster,' he said. 'Only the book will do.'

I explained this to Barry who suggested I go and get the book, which I had brought to the museum in order to make the photocopy. After retrieving it, I opened it at the relevant place, the poem in Spanish on one page and in English on the other, and handed it to Barry. 'It's a fake,' the sculptor muttered playfully, out of earshot of everyone but me, as he replaced the photocopy with the book. By this I think he meant that the poem was borrowed: yet there was no fakery here, rather a type of transcription that leads ultimately to the repossession of the model. All intellectual property is time-shared. And Colinas was right, the book made a much better component of the assembly in its own right: the poem's theme, contrasting sculptural longevity with human decay, hidden to the museum visitor unless they approached and read, was a form of added value.

By this time I had grown conscious of the aftermath of the night before, a state of affairs amplified by the events of the afternoon. We had two vans at our disposal and the first, the sleek white Volkswagen, blew a tyre on the way back to Santa Eulalia. Changing the wheel

8 *Light on light on sacks* (1969) is in the collection at S.M.A.K, Ghent, Belgium. Flanagan used the components to make different versions of the work. 'Version 5' was shown in Ibiza.

resisted all imaginary solutions and the problem was only resolved when we borrowed a jack at a nearby garage from a *simpatico* mechanic. Reaching town, we found the other van, a spacious Ebro ideal for the transport of the remaining pieces, had disappeared. We assumed it had been stolen but then located it two hours later in a back street where Barry had parked it the night before.

The day of the exhibition dawned with no sign of Barry at our usual meeting place. I walked to the studio flat where his mother Monica lived but she told me she had seen no sign of him. (I recalled the time he had visited Japan for seven weeks and reputedly come back with a dress to fit a twelve-year-old for his daughter who was five, having believed the weeks were years.) By now in a state of some alarm, I phoned the museum and to my relief Elena informed me Barry was indeed there, but strictly incommunicado.

Fifty minutes later I found myself in the downstairs gallery, standing over the sculptor. He was stretched out fully clothed on a couch, like a pharaoh surrounded by his treasures. For all I knew he had kept a nightlong vigil with them. I did not wake him, but after a few moments his eyelashes fluttered open and he leapt to his feet. His movements were jerky and disconnected as he began filling the Chinese cabinet that had been collected from his mother's and delivered early that morning. On the top of the cabinet he mounted the beautiful head of a young woman, carved in clay at the beginning of the 1960s but only recently cast in bronze. The woman's hair was drawn back and her eyes were slanted, the sockets vacant, like those of an Egyptian goddess – it is no accident that Barry was working on the set of Cleopatra when this was made.

Inside the cabinet, on the top shelf, he placed two pinch pots modelled in his primitive style. Behind these, he laid a Nijinski hare.[9] (He had a few small ones made and liked to carry one in his pocket and pull it out at appropriate moments, admiring the patina.) It was one of four hares in the show: a prancing hare and then two hares facing each other on a common platform, holding what appeared to be easels and wearing headdresses, all rendered in mild steel. Barry placed the Nijinski to the rear of the cabinet, where it remained as discreetly positioned as the label on a Savile Row suit.

On the middle shelf he rested the immaculately finished bronze heads of his two small children, between which he placed *Bes*,

The name can be taken as a homage to Rodin's similarly titled piece, but the hare's stance is more that of a karate fighter. The idea came to Barry on Ibiza and it is one of the most successful and dynamic of all the hares.

moulded in thick slabs of clay that looked as though they had been slapped together. The lowest shelf was reserved for *The Old Man of the Sea*, a large stone found on a beach, possibly at Beer in Devon, whose implacable features Barry had carved in 1958 when he was seventeen. This was so heavy that it took both of us to heave it into place.

'Thirsty?' Barry asked when this was done. I was, and hungry too, so we went to Comidas San Juan where we had a slap-up lunch of fish soup, squid and much white wine. We even tried the *pudin*, a sweet concoction similar to crème caramel but thicker. Afterwards we went to the bar on the waterfront for coffee and brandy. Barry seemed to be in a mellow mood and I decided it was a good moment to broach the possibility of some reward for my services.

'Of course, for me this has been an experience of immense interest,' I began.

Barry regarded me through hooded eyes. With his sallow skin he resembled a salamander, an impression accentuated by the way his tongue flicked across his lips, licking up any truant drops of alcohol. I had the feeling he had heard this sort of thing before.

'Costing you much in time, is it?'

'It's taken up a bit, yes,' I said, surprised to have got him down to earth so quickly.

'How many hours would you say?'

This was the crux of the matter. Did I include the many convivial times I had spent with him like this in bars and restaurants with Barry almost invariably picking up the tab? It was like setting a price on friendship.

'Thirty hours,' I suggested, a relatively modest sum in view of the fact that preparation for the exhibition had taken up the best part of a month.

'That's about three hundred thousand, isn't it?'

I could scarcely believe my ears. This was the equivalent of about fifty pounds an hour – a princely rate, far better than my usual one.

'My generation,' said Barry, suddenly lurching off on an entirely different topic, 'was taught to turn everything on its head. It's interesting to throw things up into the air and see which way they land.'

I nodded like an android. I was still thinking of the three hundred thousand. Turned on its head that made three pesetas.

'Your generation, on the other hand, threw everything up into the air and then just left it there. What did you expect to hold it up … TELEPATHY?'

The old men playing cards in their berets and crumpled check shirts glanced up from their card game and then returned to it. Not for the first time I was grateful for the remarkable tolerance the locals had for noise. Barry was glaring at me with a hostile gleam in his hazel-flecked eyes.

He was twelve years older than me and the 1950s had moulded his teenage years pretty much as the 1960s had mine. His was a youth of jazz clubs, Beat poetry in cafés, sandals and beards, whereas mine had consisted of psychedelic all-nighters at Middle Earth in platform-heeled cerise boots and henna-dyed hair, the longer the better. Barry, of course, had not been unaffected by all this and had attended many of the pivotal counter-cultural events of the 1960s, including the first International Poetry Incarnation at the Royal Albert Hall with Allen Ginsberg and Gregory Corso, which some see as the birth of the London underground. Pink Floyd had projected *Speak*, a film by John Latham, behind their live set at the launch of *International Times* at the Roundhouse in October 1966. (The unreleased soundtrack, *John Latham*, is the holy grail of the group's collectors.) Still, I always felt Barry was more of a beatnik and said something airy along the lines that we had just been guests at different venues in bohemia. Barry tut-tutted as I spoke, making me realize that despite wine and spirits his mental razor was as sharp as ever and eager to slice through any bullshit. Stressing correspondences was a little perilous – the fact that our mothers were from Liverpool, for example, or that we both had had roving theatrical childhoods and then a variety of improbable short-term jobs. Barry relished his uniqueness.

'If you play tennis with me,' he said, 'you better lob a decent ball.'

'Of course, my generation were unrealistic and a bit arrogant,' I admitted. 'We thought we had stumbled on a great secret and were the first to do so. We didn't realize there was an entire centuries-old tradition, albeit heterodox, but a tradition.'

'Getting you anywhere, is it?'

'The tradition?'

'No, living here?'

Apart from my involvement with him, the frisson it gave of art and fame and a wider world, Ibiza was starting to seem like a very small pond indeed. I told him this.

'Don't pay homage to a dead weight!' he said, in a rare allusion to my personal situation.

'And you,' I asked, 'are you progressing?'

'Swimming against the current.'

'The island was very different when I first lived here in the 1970s,' I said. 'There really was a magic. But the older generation are dying now, the ones who accepted the crazed skinny-dipping hippies without batting an eyelid, charged minuscule rents and just shrugged their shoulders and said 'Sah' when you told them you couldn't pay it. In their place you have people who want computer games for their children and bigger four-wheel drives. Everywhere has become homogenized by greed. The remaining foreigners – not the expats who are more or less identical to those you'd find in Nerja or Estepona – are like students at an art school who will never leave.'

'Hornsey-by-Sea,' muttered Barry acidly, referring to a famous bastion of student rebellion in the 1960s.

Suddenly it occurred to me that despite the sluggish siesta-inducing heat of the afternoon and the spirits we had consumed on top of so much wine, the sculptor and I were engaged in a perfectly normal conversation. I did not have to lean forward, straining to make out phrases that made no sense even when I could hear them. There were no loud exclamations, no sudden introduction of baffling names or incidents from the past. It seemed a good moment to strike.

'Should I write down my expenses as well as the hours on a sort of invoice or something?' I enquired.

'Oh, of course, the cheque,' said Barry. He reached his right hand into the inside pocket of his jacket, where he usually kept his wallet as well as letters and other papers. A look of alarm crossed his features, which intensified as his hand reached across and searched the other equally empty pocket. He flapped his hands against his two side pockets, frowning as he did so, then felt inside them. They also yielded nothing but a pencil and a packet of Marlboro. He must have left his wallet at the museum.

'I'll go up there, if you like,' I offered.

'Yes, why don't you? Someone must be there,' he nodded, sweat from the exertion of his recent hunt beading his brow. Eager as Sancho Panza, I started to make my way out of the bar but at the door he called me back.

'Can you lend me a couple of quid? '

I reached into the top pocket of my denim shirt and handed him its contents, some change and a couple of green thousand-peseta notes, which the Spanish called lettuces. Then I raced up the hill and surmised after much futile knocking on the heavy wooden door that the museum staff had all gone home for their siesta. I returned to the bar. The old men were still sitting at their table playing cards but Barry had gone. It was half past four. I had another three peseta-less hours to kill before the start of the show.

# 9

IN THE PERIOD we were working on the hang, a young English journalist called Paul Richardson appeared on Ibiza. He interviewed Barry for a book called *Not Part of the Package*, which, as the name implies, is about the side of Ibiza that tourists do not usually see. In it he describes meeting Barry at M&M's. Barry 'was sitting alone, being a little early for a rendezvous with the man he calls his 'spontaneous fixer', an unpublished author of three novels including one set on Ibiza in Roman times.' The man, of course, was me. Barry's description of my role seemed apt, though I was rather put out by the 'unpublished author' bit, despite it being no more than the truth.

Barry tells Richardson that he came to Ibiza to be a father. 'Was it a good place for that?' Richardson asks. 'No!' Barry replies. 'It's a good place to be a mother.' Barry then goes on to speak dismissively of the derivative nature of the local art scene and the lack of any real support system for artists on the island. 'Ibiza's got no middle class,' he says. In other words, you needed to have your network and reputation in place before you came to the island. This was certainly Barry's case and explains the exceptional turnout on the exhibition's first night.

When I reached the museum at eight, I was immediately struck by the unusual number of cars parked alongside the walls of the bulwark and by the throngs of people sauntering in the same direction as me. The upper gallery with its unremarkable display of graphic art was not so crowded, but going downstairs I saw people were queuing to get into the left-hand gallery, which hosted Barry's art. When I did get in, I noticed there were two distinct groups. The first was Spanish and composed of the museum regulars, which included gallery owners, local journalists, pundits and civil servants from the town hall, which had put up the funding. The latter were attired more formally then the rest, the men in suits and ties, the women in evening dresses. They exuded an air of ownership, as though they had authored the show themselves, but as I passed the small groups they stood huddled in I picked up not one reference to the extraordinary work on show; instead, they were griping about bosses or gossiping about colleagues. I saw Elena deep in conversation with the mayor, a man with a moustache and a tweed jacket, which he wore despite the heat. Moving on, I made eye contact with one of the journalists who had been at the press conference.

'Remarkable work,' he said, coming up to me, 'a grand day for the museum. It is so of the home, so novel.' His voice seemed to have gone down an octave and he was sniffling. 'Sorry, I am constipated.' It seemed indelicate to inform him that the Spanish *constipado* and its English doppelganger refer to opposite ends of the body. 'Above everything I am most impressing for the *sacos*. It is a witty illusion.'

He was referring to the mound of sacks taking up one corner of the gallery with the rectangle of light hovering on the wall above them like a doorway that could take you through to another dimension, perhaps the one that Barry truly inhabited. This had its fair share of admirers, including several children. As Colinas had observed, while he sat giggling with Elena on these same sacks that morning, it was a show for everyone – the very young as well as the very old.

The children were drawn from the second contingent there that night, the foreign community, some rich, some poor, several self-proclaimed artists like myself, all united by the fact that they had settled on the island as an escape route from the stressful world outside. There were women in multi-coloured crocheted dresses wearing misshapen hats with feathers or pieces of ripe fruit attached to their rims. With them were men in outsize jackets with dreamy faces. I saw Lance Tilbury, the English painter, wearing the green velvet smoking jacket Terry-Thomas had given him with a lily in one buttonhole. Lance had come up to the museum a couple of times that week and had helped with the hang. He was holding forth about the work to an attentive crowd.

'Snapper!' he said, employing the nickname inspired by my aggressive strikes at the ball when playing billiards. 'Barry's been asking for you. He's over there on the pyramid with his mummy.'

I did not recall our bringing any pyramids into the gallery, but as I neared the left-hand bay that Lance had indicated, I realized he meant the piece in mild steel that took up much of it. Barry was sitting on the circular base with his soles resting on the thick flakes of salt that ringed the piece. It occurred to me that the *Homage* might make a new type of park bench; the only objection to this being the Jarry-esque symbol, which could evoke in those with evil minds the image of a penis and balls. Barry had changed into a dark suit made up of a short jacket and billowing trousers. Beneath the jacket he was wearing a white t-shirt. He seemed fresh and rested. Sitting on a stool facing him was an old woman with a craggy face and glasses. She was wearing a long dress and smoking a cigarette. This was Monica, the sculptor's mother.

'It's all gone rather smoothly, don't you think?' said Barry.

For Frances
through Fox
July 15/72 PP

# 10

THE EXHIBITION RECEIVED rave notices in the local press and it was decided to extend it until the end of August. There was one unexpected downside to such longevity, however: rats infiltrated the museum, discovered the sacks in the basement, and being no respecters of modern art, made a feast out of their contents.

One day in high summer Barry sidled up to me in M&M's. After deciphering the hieroglyphics, I realized the exhibition was being transferred to Palma and he was inviting me along for the ride. We had by now settled the more mercenary side of our dealings. I had valued my services at forty thousand pesetas a month, and he had given me this and a large, Jarry-esque drawing of Foxy on beige paper. Unusually, he had painted the swollen curves with watercolour and ink. On line with the image's right foot Barry had written, 'For Francis through Fox' and beneath this '15 July 1992' in reddish-brown ink. The dedicatee was Francis Bacon and the date the day of his death.

OPPOSITE
*For Francis through Fox*, 1992,
Ink on paper

Foxy, the self-styled 'Queen of Soho' knew both artists, but I was not sure of any connection between Barry and Bacon, though they had frequented the same haunts, such as the French House and the Colony Club. According to Barry's friend Kevin Whitney (Olympic painter and maker in his youth of a psychedelic film featuring Syd Barrett) Barry had been drinking champagne with an art dealer one day in Groucho's when a fierce row had ensued after the dealer had accused Barry of coming from a privileged background. (Barry had gone to a public school in Sussex, but if he belonged to any class, it was strictly the bohemian one.) The argument grew so heated that Barry picked up the full champagne bottle, upturned it, placed it in the bucket and stormed out. It was at that point that Francis Bacon, drinking at the bar, enquired who he was.

On Monday, 14 September 1992, I met Barry at Ibiza airport. He was wearing his dark green Armani suit, now dusty and long overdue for a visit to the dry cleaner's, and three of his front teeth were missing, a development he did not care to explain. He was truly full of surprises that day and Magdalena Aguilo, the curator at Sala de Cultura, the gallery hosting the exhibition in Palma, seemed quite surprised by our arrival, as the show was not due to start until one week later. I wondered if Barry had confused the dates but he just made oblique references to two individuals he needed to find on Mallorca without specifying who they were.

The gallery had booked us into the Palladium, a mid-range hotel for business travellers that neither of us liked. Barry spent much of the evening phoning and sending faxes. Recession had been hitting the market hard. Now it seemed there was to be a further tightening of the screw. Britain's position in the European Exchange Rate Mechanism was becoming unsustainable due to the unrealistically high rate the pound had been pegged at against the Deutschmark, which had impacted in a devastating way on employment and exports. Sales of Barry's work were diving. Moreover, A & A Sculpture Casting, his foundry in the East End, had been in jeopardy for some time, both because of the general economic gloom and problems in the partnership that ran it at that time. Barry was business-like and sober in his dealings, and after a night of what the Irish politely call the *craic*, I saw him switch into executive mode and hold a highly detailed and precise telephone conversation with his gallery owner, Leslie Waddington, as though accountant's ink, not whisky, flowed through his veins.

The next morning we had a quick breakfast, checked out, and went off in search of a hire car. Barry, it seemed, wanted to tour the island, which I found perplexing as tourism for its own sake never seemed to be his thing. The streets were busy with shoppers jostling in the sunshine and there was that mingled aroma of fresh coffee and hair oil that pervades Spanish cities. We rented a car and drove out of the city heading west. I had not a clue why we were doing this or where we were going. It was about forty minutes later, when the hills were rising all around us, that we coined the term 'invertigo' for a new type of phobia – Barry's fear of being dwarfed by mountains.

Reaching Valldemossa, we drove past stalls cluttered with miniature pianos and George Sands' account of the winter she spent with Chopin on Mallorca, printed in twenty different languages. The entire town, with its dinky houses swathed in red or purple bougainvillea, was a shrine to the composer. (Ironically, he had loathed the place during his six-month stay, finding the winter dampness only served to worsen the tuberculosis that would kill him.) We parked in the main square, which was full of German or Japanese tourists, and had a lunch of tough chicken and chips at an outside table of that type of local restaurant the locals never go to.

For some time I had been struck by the fact that Barry seemed to do very little work. On Ibiza days passed with the sculptor ambling about the house in his kimono and sandals, occasionally fiddling with a bit of wire or scribbling on the wall next to the fireplace. Most of his energy seemed to be reserved for bars. It had not always been like this. I had described my own fight with sloth: the battle to force myself to start writing in the mornings. He told me that when young he used to sleep with two alarm clocks on the table next to him and one under the pillow. So, in what I thought was a subtle way, I would gently chide him for his current inactivity and speak of the therapeutic nature of occupation – work as its own reward. This was of course incredibly ignorant and presumptuous of me. That summer alone Barry had a dozen large sculptures at the Yorkshire Sculpture Park, in a show called The Names of the Hare, as well as an exhibition consisting of bronzes at the Durand-Desert gallery in Paris. Nevertheless, my sermonizing on the joys of the Puritan work ethic must have struck a chord, because after lunch he disappeared for a couple of hours, leaving me with two Camels and a *carajillo* for company. On his return, he opened his pad and showed me a wonderful sketch he had made of the local monastery. Apart from being a thing of beauty, it exhibited in the employment of line, shade and perspective, a devastating technical mastery. It was precisely because he had the virtuosity to render something as classical as this that Barry could demolish the foundations and lay a piece of rope or a heap of sand on a floor and make them art as well.

After Valldemossa, we took the winding road and drove through Deya, where I had stayed a couple of times during the years between sojourns on Ibiza. I had been looking for a substitute for the White Island and had hoped to find it in the mountain village, which possessed some similarities. This went swimmingly until the day I ran into a German hippie called Gipsy, whom had I had known on Ibiza before he had been thrown off the island. 'Deya is a replica,' he told me. Kevin Ayers of Soft Machine lived there as well as Lady June, the Beat poetess, whom I had met in London. Most famously, of course, it was the home for many years of Robert Graves, who, with his white-goddess lore and advocacy of magic mushrooms as a rite of passage into adulthood, was a hero to my younger self. I told Barry the story of Graves jumping out of the first-floor window of the London flat he shared with the American poetess Laura Riding after discovering her in bed with an Irish lover. Laughter acted on the sculptor's shoulders like a pump. 'At least he didn't jump into bed with them,' he chuckled.

That night we stayed in a large hotel built before the Civil War in Puerto de Soller, which evoked Agatha Christie and a less hurried age. In the morning we set off for Pollensa, which lies on the northwestern tip of the island. Crags stubbled with patches of vegetation and squat, wind-contorted trees lined both sides of the road. 'This much stone could give a sculptor indigestion,' observed Barry. This was droll but otherwise he seemed preoccupied. In fact, that same day, known from then on as Black Wednesday, the markets ejected the UK from the ERM and the pound went into free fall.

We discovered this later when Barry telephoned London from his room in the spa hotel we checked into in Pollensa. More crushing for the sculptor than the news of the financial crash was that the foundry was going into liquidation. 'I need somebody to give me a job,' he said. But his good humour did not desert him for long. Sleek and relaxed, he lounged on a reclining leather armchair in a dark kimono sipping Jameson from the room bar. Suddenly I saw not the poet of the building site or the hobo of Ibiza but the artist-star who kept a room on permanent standby at The Chelsea Hotel in New York. This was the globally renowned sculptor who had the quiet satisfaction of knowing everything he owned or gave away – every cocktail, gourmet meal and property – had been produced by the sweat of his brow, if not always of his hands. 'In my youth I made something out of nothing,' as he would put it.

The spa hotel had a number of pools with channels opening onto the Mediterranean. In the morning the health-conscious, predominantly German guests dived into them with the determination of penguins, but we set off again on our mysterious mission, taking the road that skirted the coast and then headed inland. Eventually, we reached Arta, a pleasant town, so off the tourist track it boasted only one hotel. I had read that Princess Diana owned a house there and for a moment entertained the wild notion that Barry might be bent on a secret assignation. The sculptor appeared to be a bit muddled at this point and disappeared into a phone booth. We had missed our turn-off it seemed, which we only regained after driving back along the road we had come on. The turning led us to a dark hill with a solitary house nestling beneath it. We drove through the gate and parked in the driveway. The road continued until it met a cluster of distant roofs beside a sparkling sea. A wiry man came out of the house. He had an aquiline nose and a wide smile that displayed his teeth. He shook hands with Barry, who turned to me and announced, 'This is Miquel.' There was something enticing about the place at the end of the road – the arrangement of coast and sea glistening in the sunlight. I asked its name. Our host told us and said there was a good *pensione* there. I resolved to visit it one day.

The house had a living area with comfortable chairs. A woman came in, blonde, lithe, not seeming Spanish; she was, in fact, Miquel's Dutch wife. She nodded to us and went out again to where a baby was crying. Miquel, it seemed, had recently become a father and we congratulated him. He offered coffee and we accepted. Our host had only little English and Barry few words of Spanish so at times it was necessary for me to put on my interpreter's hat, which was full of holes. Still brooding on the collapse of his foundry, Barry started talking about alternatives, and a discussion ensued on the relative merits of Clementi's in Paris and another establishment in Barcelona. This seemed to lead naturally to talk of quarries, an obsession of Barry's and also it turned out of Miquel's, who described with animation various types of stone that could be found on Mallorca: the sandstone of Petra and high quality onyx from the Caves of Hams.

Unexpectedly, Barry mentioned I was a writer, a description I was not all that comfortable with as I had little to show for it – 'aspired to be' might have been a better way of putting it. This excited Miquel's interest. Like Barry he nursed a friendly rivalry with writers and told us he would have liked to have become one himself. He had in fact established a friendship with Paul Bowles, American author of *The Sheltering Sky*, in Africa. 'I'm a good reader but a bad writer,' he declared in English and asked me what I was working on. I told him about my novel set on Ibiza in Roman times and this got him talking about the island. He used to catch the ferry to Ibiza town in the mid 1970s and just hang out, savouring, as I had, the heady kaleidoscope of freedom and new forms of experience suddenly on offer after the long night of Franco's Spain. I told him I had sold Spanish foreign legion surplus at the market in Es Canar, olive-green trousers with deep pockets and khaki shirts. He said he had gone there often too, when it really had been a hippie market.

Miquel was a purposeful man with not much time for small talk and of course Barry rarely had any either. Our host ran a hand through his spiky hair, rose nimbly to his feet and asked if we would like to see the studio. This turned out to be a light, airy, industrial-sized space, one entire wall of which was taken up by a half-finished canvas. It was a blitz of colour, with paint applied so thickly that parts of it formed a three-dimensional hybrid between painting and sculpture. Other canvases leaning against the wall displayed a more figurative bent. The first of one stack bore the expressive head of a donkey.

'Here the light changes every ten minutes,' Miquel said, 'but in Paris it's constant.'

The painter explained he only spent about a third of the year on Mallorca; in what sounded an enviable arrangement, he divided the rest of the time between Paris and Mali. There was an old poster for an exhibition peeling from a wall, which supplied his surname – Barceló, Miquel Barceló – and so furnished the last piece of the jigsaw.

Now in his mid-thirties, he had hung out with Andy Warhol in 1980s New York, befriended Jean-Michel Basquiat, and become an object of desire for the world's leading galleries when he exhibited at Documenta 7, in Kassel, Germany, in 1982. Curiously, Barry, sixteen years his senior, had achieved international recognition in the same year when he represented Britain at the Venice Biennale. Both born in January, the two artists also possessed nomadic souls, a tendency to use animals as subjects and a deep reverence for materials, many of them unconventional. In Africa, where the previous year he had built a floating studio and sailed down the Niger, Miquel happily employed local soil in his canvases and then let termites finish off the job. In Mallorca, he was as likely as not to incorporate a pig's skull or work with an industrial paint sprayer. This mirrored Barry's shamanic use of sacking and rope to cast his spells. Yet there seemed to be a precision and order to Miquel's practice – the immaculate house, the organized globetrotting itinerary, the uncluttered studio – at variance with Barry's shambolic arrangements on Ibiza. The painter did not appear to be such a child of chaos as the sculptor, who, at least during that period, embraced turmoil and so was energized, sometimes against the odds.

We went outside and Miquel introduced us to four of his models: donkeys of a breed indigenous to Mallorca. In fact, everything we could see came from the island. With a wide sweep his hand took in a sty, from which native black pigs with conical snouts and redundant neck glands greeted us with honks; minuscule European palm trees, only found on Mallorca; and the stubborn hill, home to fierce Mallorquin bulls, that receded into the distance like a fist when we drove away later.

The road taking us back to Palma ran parallel with a disused railway line where wild flowers peeked out between the sleepers. We stopped in a town in the centre of the Mallorca called Sineu and had squid and lamb washed down with a good red wine from Léon. The sculptor seemed pleased with our visit.

'Miquel's got a head just like Picasso's,' he declared.

Barry had made similar references to people's anatomy before. I assumed he was speaking from a sculptural point of view. It was rare, however, that the artist's words confined themselves to one interpretation only. Was he referring to the shape of the painter's head or to what was in it?

Untitled, 1996.
Portrait of Barry
Flanagan by
Miquel Barceló.
Mixed media,
28 ³/₄" x 21 ¹/₄" /
73 x 54cm

# 11

BARRY HAD LOATHED the Palladium ever since we had come across a bar called the Yuppie around the corner from the hotel, so on our return to the city we looked for sleeping quarters in the more congenial warren of narrow streets and old alleys that lie in the port zone and constitute Palma's Ramblas, where the other person Barry was hunting was more likely to be found. 'If he isn't dead,' the sculptor added in a whisper that cried out for the stage. Just off the main drag there were a couple of *pensiones* in a cobbled street lined with every style of restaurant from Galician to English. Next door to the clean and decent but fully booked Savoy was a particularly squalid and rundown affair with a squint-eyed man at the desk. This is where we checked in.

The god of exits and entrances had heard Barry, however. Making our way down an alley that led to the sea the next morning, we ran into a short emaciated man who started when he saw us. I had known Tony since the 1970s. He had sensual lips, curly black hair greying at the edges, and shiny skin that seemed to be too tightly stretched over his face. It was serendipity we had found him, he told us in fluent hipster English. He had just been released from hospital, where he had spent the last twenty-five days. His left ear was swollen and a large pad of cotton wool adhered to it. The doctor thought he had a tumour.

Tony led us back down to the street where we were staying, except instead of turning right in the direction of our *pensione*, we took a left down an alley. We paused beside the peeling grey wall of one of the houses. He pointed upwards towards an overhanging balcony and told us that was the flat he shared with his mother. It was a warm morning. Blue was deepening in a sky streaked by feathery cloud. We followed Tony to the nearest bar, the Café Metropol.

We made an incongruous threesome: Tony, with his staring, pitch-black eyes and perversely shiny skin, decked out in a blue collarless Indian shirt and baggy trousers from the same continent; Barry in the dark green Armani suit, with white shirt undone at the collar and striped tie; me in a blue denim shirt and black chinos. Compared to the others on the terrace, however, we were as inconspicuous as the cumbersome pigeons who pecked at each other as they squabbled over crumbs on the cobblestones. On a table to our left was a bearded man with a sallow face and cunning eyes wearing a peaked nautical cap. He was swilling beer directly from the bottle. Behind him a pair of men sat at a table with their backs leaning against the wall. There in the blameless sunlight I felt a type of dread I had rarely known on Ibiza. We were in a Fagin's kitchen of junkies and petty thieves, who lounged in the sun like lizards when not darting off on sinister missions. Everyone, including the women, tipsy in their shiny PVC miniskirts and stilettos, with uncomely bodies that were bartered for drugs, seemed to know Tony and greeted him as they passed.

'These are my friends from Ibiza,' Tony called out to a passing man with greasy locks and a ripped brown leather jacket.

'Ibiza's finished!' the man hissed back.

'I want to go to India to die,' Tony said, looking directly at Barry. 'They shoot barbiturates round here when there isn't any smack. I need ginseng. They give you anything in hospital, uppers, downers, but never ginseng.'

A portly waiter with smiling eyes brought out a tray with two bottles of San Miguel, which he carefully poured into iced glasses, and a tubular glass, three-quarters full of whisky and ice. Barry, who never liked ice in his drink but usually embarked on a long ritual as to the precise measure of water, said nothing.

'Where's the sitar, Tony?' I asked as I took a sip of the cold beer.

'I was playing a lot in the summer round Plaza de la Reina. Some nights I got twenty-five thousand pesetas from the tourists but I spent it all on smack. I've still got the sitar but I want to sell it so I can go to India.'

We parted from Tony, who was not hungry, soon afterwards and had lunch at a restaurant in a little alleyway that led to a quarter called La Lonja, where the old fish market had been. 'Lonja' means rasher of bacon and is a good description of the zone, which is shaped like a strip. Ostensibly a pizzeria, the restaurant had a *menu del día* with many choices, and the food was good. We both started with thick garlic soup. 'Good for the blood,' said Barry. Then I progressed to kidneys in a sherry sauce, which was served in a brown ceramic bowl, while Barry had chicken and red peppers. For sweet there was the Mallorcan version of *pudin*, resembling the one on Ibiza but thicker and creamier. With the black coffees we ordered they left a full bottle of Veterano and two brandy glasses. By the time Barry left, the bottle was half empty. I stayed put, finishing off the rest of the bottle, which seemed to be complimentary as nobody came out to charge me. I was intoxicated not only by the drink but by the hot square of blue sky framed between the roofs above, through which the gulls wheeled in dizzying arcs.

: : : : : : : : : : : : : : : :

Barry came to see me around seven. My room was bare except for two single beds with one bedside table, a sink and a cupboard. The window opened inwards onto a central shaft in which all the smells and noises in the building seemed to congregate.

'Madame X is coming over from Ibiza. I'll probably be occupied with her all weekend,' Barry told me, flashing a tooth-missing smile. 'You better take this for some watercolours and Tony's ginseng or whatever.' He laid a five thousand note on one of the tables and, almost as an afterthought, added a blue ten thousand one. 'Oh, by the way, the Savoy has two rooms available so I'm taking one for myself and another for her.'

He seemed uncomfortable, and though my reaction was as non-committal as I could make it, I felt like a servant told to sleep in the stables while the master takes the best room in the inn. But what could I do? I was not calling the shots.

We went out and found a congenial-looking café and sat at a table on the terrace. The market building opposite had been constructed in the same gothic style as the cathedral and there was an angel above the entrance, which did not seem to disapprove of the fact that we had switched to Russian vodka splashed with tonic. We downed a few in quick succession. The evening was still and warm. A sickle moon dimpled the sky. I listened as Barry confessed to a preoccupation with the lack of new work he was producing. He was still trading on themes developed in the early 1980s and so pronounced was his aura that he could get away with it. It was, after all, the dawn of an era when few looked beyond celebrity to the work itself. The square was filling up and I was surprised at the number of attractive women. Much the better for the vodka, we toured the area and had several more in various establishments. There were oyster bars and art-nouveau cafés with wide windows filled with chattering Friday night throngs that spilled out onto the pavement. We ended up in a bar facing the Metropol where we had spent the morning with Tony.

Barry and I had been getting along famously. Made exuberant by vodka, I babbled on, quoting poetry and parading my useless knowledge of quirky word origins. Drink turned me into a flatterer and I complimented him on the fact that such was his talent success had been inevitable, but Barry had worked very hard and my praise did not seem to have the required effect. The salamander was with us: the sculptor's tongue darted to and fro across lips as ashen as his face.

'Let's get up to date,' he barked. 'How much is it so far?'

I tried to explain in my puppyish way how difficult it was to put a figure on what to me was not a job but a friendship. This annoyed him and he started to repeat 'up to date' like a mantra. Very well then, I thought, and I confessed that what I was really looking for was a type of sinecure, something steady, a modest stipend paid monthly over a year or so in order that I might finish my book. This only served to infuriate him further. 'I know what you're after,' he shouted, 'I know your little game. Why don't you go back? Piss off! Get the plane tomorrow!'

Everyone was looking at us now. I got up, walked outside, and went some way down a narrow alley. Barry followed me, pushed me against a wall and began slapping me. The slaps were light and tickled more than stung, but I pushed him away and made my way back to the *pensione*. In my seedy room with its rancid smells and dull flickering light I fell asleep fully clothed on the bed.

An indeterminate time later a loud banging awoke me and I opened the door. There stood Barry hopping from one foot to another with fury.

'You've got my LIGHTER!' he bellowed.

I knew I hadn't and told him so, but he tried to force his way into the room. I pushed him out, calling him a bloody idiot as I did so. He repeated the words as though he had never heard such effrontery. His room was directly beneath mine and he was still repeating them when he went back to it. 'Bloody idiot! He called me a bloody idiot!' and then he began to rave hoarsely and relentlessly. I drifted in and out of sleep, the raving echoing up the shaft.

Late the next morning I asked the squint-eyed concierge about 'my friend'. He had checked out early it seemed.

'Lots of shouting last night,' the concierge muttered. 'Came from the room below yours. But I'd be careful about the son of a bitch on the same floor as you. He seems to be barking as well!'

# 12

IT WAS PAST eleven when I went to the Metropol and joined Tony, who was drinking coffee from a glass and gazing at the square. I was badly hung over and as I shakily carried a beer from the bar I had second thoughts about being there. There was the same cast of junkies as the day before but in my parlous state they seemed doubly sinister. Tony asked how Barry was. I briefly related what had happened.

'I should go back to Ibiza,' I declared. I had an open ticket but apart from what Barry had given me the previous evening (which I felt duty-bound to spend on Tony) I had very little money.

'It will blow over,' Tony said. 'He has a temper. You have to bear with him.'

Before we left Ibiza Barry had been interviewed by Victoria Combalía, a well-known art critic who wrote for *El País*. Her piece was due to appear today. Dutifully, I bought a copy of the paper and found her full-page article, entitled 'Artefactos Serios' ('Serious Artefacts'), illustrated with some hares and an elephant from the current show in Paris. She began by describing Barry's life on Ibiza and went on to elaborate on the transition he had made from his early creations in hessian and sand to the playful hares with their immense commercial appeal. Combalía displayed a genuine appreciation in the article and I thought Barry would relish her words, especially the conclusion that found a disconcerting yet intriguing quality in his work. I wondered if I would get the chance to tell him about it.

On cue I noticed the great man crossing the square. He was looking spruce in a short grey jacket and was with an aristocratic-looking woman with an attractive face whose most pronounced features were a prominent nose and wavy auburn hair. She had a shapely body beneath her loose silk dress and glided along the cobblestones in pale pink espadrilles. Despite the pandemonium of the night before, Barry also carried himself with a jaunty air. Tony and I both recognized the woman. She had been on Ibiza since the 1970s and sold Balinese clothes at the Saturday market at Las Dalias. Resisting the impulse to rush over and wave the newspaper article in its subject's face I said, 'So that's Madame X.'

Seeing the woman prompted Tony to talk more about the past, when he had travelled the world with drugs stashed on him everywhere. There was always a chick or three, and he was beautiful with curly hair and a bronzed, unravaged body. In everything he described there was greed – for pleasure, for fucks, for hits. He had been as selfish as all of us; though he believed Shiva would absolve him when he got to India, which he was sure he would do with Barry's money.

We left the bar and crossing the square a couple staggered past us. It was difficult to tell if they were fighting or canoodling because they screamed at each other and laughed almost simultaneously. She was stoned already, but there was something eager in their stance that told you they were off to fuck or fix. We took a taxi and went uptown to the commercial district. Just past the Palladium, Tony told the driver, whom he seemed to know, to take a narrow street, and we passed an ironmonger's and then a haberdasher's with striking art nouveau façades. The taxi drew up beside a down-at-heel apartment block with peeling walls. Tony asked me for some money. I gave him a two thousand bill, but he said it was not enough. Assuming he was going into one of the shops, I asked if the money was for the watercolours I knew Barry wanted, but he shrugged and repeated that it was not enough. I peeled off another bill and he got out of the taxi, disappeared, and soon came back. He said something to the driver and we drove to another street and a shop that did indeed sell artist's materials. I put out some more of Barry's money for a set of watercolours and did not ask what the other stop had been about, except I was certain it was not ginseng.

On Sunday Tony took me to his mother's flat. Thankfully, she was out. He fed me mussels, cheese and a tart his sister had brought. Again he talked of India and of the past while his battered sitar, with strings missing and a dent on one side, gazed forlornly at us from the wall it leant against. I felt sorry for Tony's mother, who had to watch him die.

The next morning the concierge told me there was a message from 'my friend': I should move to the Savoy next door. I realized I was back on board and this came as a relief. It was not only money that had stopped me returning to Ibiza. Presumptuously perhaps, I felt I had a stake in the show and its success. Moreover, I had started wondering if the whole business might be irksome for Barry: it had been a long time since he had been called upon to make so much effort for so little reward. Here he was piddling about in Palma while his business was in tatters. Sales were falling through the floor. The foundry was bust. He might have to go back to producing the Flanagan notes he had exchanged with friends for services. To top it all, his family life was in disarray: Renate had moved to another house near the road to San Miguel.

The Savoy boasted a large cobbled courtyard with a flight of steps at the end of it. Ascending these brought me face to face with a middle-aged man and a woman whose permed hair and fag in mouth fitted the role of seaside landlady to a tee. In soft American tones the man told me my room was ready and Barry had gone to the gallery.

Sala de Cultura belonged to Sa Nostra, a Spanish savings bank that subsidized a range of artistic activities. It was situated off Palma's main shopping street in a zone of galleries and opulent shops and bars. The curator, the self-possessed woman with chestnut hair who had treated us so briskly when we first arrived before our trip in search of Barceló, was at the gallery with Barry. There did not seem to have been much of a thawing in their relations. Mine with the sculptor's was much improved, however. Barry greeted me with a wink and a whispered 'Flexibility of the bond is true economy.'

We toured the three large first-floor rooms that comprised the gallery. Once more my translation skills were taxed almost beyond endurance as I tried to convey Barry's riddles. He seemed to be harbouring no grudge and rewarded me with friendly winks when the curator nodded, though more usually she seemed baffled by his pronouncements. She was also probably wondering about his teeth.

The gallery was a very different affair to the museum in Ibiza. The core of the building was early nineteenth century but a modern extension had been built on to it. Two of the three rooms belonged to the new part and were white and rectangular, lit by neon strips. The middle one, however, which faced the street, was of the original part of the building and had floral brocade wallpaper, Doric columns and intricate recesses – the room would not have looked out of place at Versailles. The exhibition was to open at 8pm the next day. The exhibits, which had been transported from Ibiza, were sprawled around the courtyard downstairs like labourers on their day off. There was not much time for the hang, which, given the layout, would be very different than on Ibiza. One key element was in place, however – the rooms allocated for Barry (one new, one old) had been carpeted wall to wall in green.

The curator had already decided the hang. Barry listened like an obedient child as I translated her instructions, whispering 'You think I should?' at regular intervals. When it got to the salt base for the mild steel *Homages*, she raised clear objections. The very whiteness of the new room, which was transparently the only possible site, would render the salt almost invisible; something darker, yet not so coarse, was called for.

'Cloth,' she suggested.

'You think I should?' said Barry.

'A fine muslin, possibly brocade,' she urged, getting so carried away it was easy to believe her true forte was textiles.

'You think I should?' said Barry.

'There is an excellent haberdasher's nearby.'

'You think I should?' said Barry.

'We could go there now.'

'You think we should?' said Barry.

So we left the gallery and were led by the curator through a square with bustling cafés and, surprisingly, a C&A, until we came to the same street of art-nouveau shops I had driven through with Tony. We entered the haberdasher's, and Barry busied himself examining cloth, finally settling on a roll of canvas, from which the assistant cut several metres. Although the curator paid with her company card she looked for a moment as though she was going to balk at the price, which must have been very high. We carried the canvas back to the gallery and laid it out against one of the *Homages* resting in the courtyard. Barry peered inscrutably at the result for a few moments. 'Shan't be using that!' he hissed to me.

There were some journalists waiting for us in the reception area. I interpreted as Barry spoke of Celts and the life of flax and hessian. After this, he disappeared for a minute, and came back with a bulging pocket. By now used to mysterious missions, I stayed mum as we hailed a taxi, which took us to a factory on the city outskirts. All of this seemed to be pre-arranged, and indeed it had been by the curator. We entered the factory and were met by a man in welding goggles. Barry fumbled in his pocket and produced the dark round head that lay on the book in *Head of the Goddess*. He handed it to the man who put it in a clamp and then, after we had looked away, applied a welding torch to it for several minutes. After allowing it to cool, during which we each had a cigarette, the welder handed the head back to Barry. The surface, with its vague suggestion of lips and a mouth, was much blacker and considerably smoother. Barry seemed satisfied and put it in his pocket.

That seemed to be enough business for the day. We had some lunch and returned to the Savoy where I was grateful for the hot shower I took and clean sheets of the bed I had a siesta in. Refreshed, I joined Barry at a downstairs bar in the early evening. He was with one of the journalists who had been at the press conference, a friendly man who took us on a tour of neighbourhood bars, at the end of which we got in a taxi and went to a late-night venue called Paris Texas, where the house drink was mescal tequila. This was the type with the worm in the bottle and both Barry and I had swallowed one before the night was over. At one point the sculptor seemed to have entered another dimension. He started dancing to music that none of us could hear, shuffling back and forth with his hands in his pockets, muttering to himself while he did so. The journalist grew concerned.

'Your friend should be careful,' he said. 'He hasn't got long if he goes on like that.'

These words, fortunately, were not to prove prophetic.

*Explic a Me,*
1994

# 13

BREAKFAST AT The Savoy was served in an enclosed patio designed to look like a space outdoors, carpeted with imitation grass. We sat on deck chairs beneath a sun umbrella and worked our way through cornflakes, eggs and bacon and tea. I said I felt like an actor staying in digs. Barry nodded and agreed he felt the same. The room was lit by a sunlamp whose glare did little for my aching head. The sunlight outside only accentuated this dismal feeling, and though I never once heard Barry complain about the aftermath of drink, he must have felt the same. It was nearly ten and we were supposed to be in the gallery on the hour. Instead, after we left the Savoy, we made a beeline for the first bar we came to on Paseo de Born and ordered that supreme hangover cure, Fernet Branca.

'I don't want cloth, I want salt,' Barry muttered as we both started on a second glass of the black, pungent restorative.

I went to the bar and asked the barman where on the entire island of Mallorca I could find such an article. He told me to try the supermarket, but I explained I wanted at least a hundredweight-worth and it had to be in the form of crystalline flakes. Puzzled, he referred the question to a group of card players busy with their game at a table near the jackpot machine. A heated discussion in Catalan ensued. After a while they came back with an authoritative answer. There were salt flats at a place called Ses Salines, which was on the extreme southern tip of the island, a mere hour and a half away by car. To cap it all, the conveyor of this information was a taxi driver. It all seemed too good to be true.

I relayed this information to Barry along with another Fernet for both of us. 'I'll take a taxi, go there and get the salt if you like,' I said. 'I should be back in time for the show.'

Barry grinned at me. He had been extraordinarily handsome when young and this had lingered into middle age. His brown eyes were hazel-flecked and his greying hair was so prone to dryness that at times it resembled fibreglass. His skin was dotted with freckles and at the chin tufts of straggly white bristle aspired to become the jazzman's beard he was currently cultivating. He was wearing his Armani suit, which must have been rather fetching and expensive when bought but now bore deep creases and sweat stains from his dancing of the night before. It looked as though he had slept in it, and he may well have done so. A grubby white sweatshirt covered half his neck, which, apart from the rip just below his Adam's apple, gave him the appearance of an eccentric yet benevolent vicar.

'I'm juggling with three balls instead of two,' he suddenly declared.

'Then throw one to me,' I suggested brightly.

'I might drop the other two!' There was a flicker of annoyance. 'My work is of the third world, if not the fourth. Yes, the fourth! You can tell them this, of the fourth world, or dimension if you prefer. Someone's got to go there.'

Then a strange thing happened. Transported in a Tardis of Fernet Branca, I entered the Flanagan dimension. My relationship with space and time altered so all at once we had fast-forwarded to late afternoon and were grinning at complicities that would have made no sense to anyone else, except perhaps the shade of Alfred Jarry. I was dimly aware that there was a hang to do, the exhibition was opening at eight and the curator must be fuming, but none of this seemed of any consequence at all. It was only when the barman affably informed us that the Fernet bottle was empty that normality reared its obtrusive and pedestrian head. This was shortly before six.

In the Flanagan dimension human flight was a reality, for in a jiffy we had reached the gallery and there was the curator frowning at us like a Salvation Army officer. Barry dropped to one knee and bent his head like a knight begging forgiveness, and for the first time she smiled. Then he sprang into action, with me and a couple of helpers laid on for the occasion scurrying around at his beck and call. Just as on Ibiza, in the twinkling of an eye he was immensely focused and when the first guests started arriving and wine and canapés were being doled out, everything was in place. It was a brilliant hang. He decided to leave the *Homages* in the courtyard, with nothing ringing their bases, and positioned *Head of the Goddess* in the central alcove at the end of the corridor that gave onto the stairs. In this way, the freshly gilded torso, dark head and book, made more of an impact than they had on Ibiza.

# 14

THE SUMMER SHOWS of 1992 produced hardly a ripple and very little in the way of hues and could be viewed as a digression from the main thrust of Barry's career – a footnote in the chronology. As Ab, the director of Barry's foundry, would tell me: 'Those exhibitions were just a sideshow. He did them to keep you and Lance happy. Leslie never even heard of them.' Lance, of course, was the English painter and long-time inhabitant of Ibiza.

A book was mooted, made up of poems by Colinas and engravings by Barry. I was to provide the English translations. The engraver, Joan Roma, was a friend of Colinas's. He lived in Barcelona and worked mainly with the celebrated Catalan artist Tàpies. The book would be produced as a collector's item in a limited edition. I visited Colinas and he gave me three poems to translate: 'El Muro Blanco', 'Ruiseñores' and 'La Ladera de Los Podencos Salvajes'. These became 'The White Wall', 'Nightingales' and 'The Mountainside of the Wild Hounds' respectively. The book would not appear until 1995 as *Pájaros en el Muro* (*Birds on the Wall*) after the engraving made of Barry's pencil drawing, whose production I had facilitated at the outset when the photo was taken.

Barry was away much of the autumn, producing ceramics at the Llorens Artigas Foundation at Gallifa in Catalonia. Artigas was a lifelong friend and collaborator of Miró and the foundation was dedicated to wood firing. Barry also had a one-man show in Montreal that year. In the following year, 1993, he participated in a show called Gravity and Grace at the Hayward Gallery, which tried to revive something of the rebellious, experimental mood of the 1960s, the 'pollenization of ideas' as he termed it. In the spring, the ceramicist Jordi Alfaro visited Ibiza and taught him how to handle glazes and critical temperatures. The highlight of the year, however, was the exhibition held in September in Madrid under the auspices of the British Council and La Caixa, the savings bank. Despite Barry declaring he did not want one until he was dead, this was a retrospective, featuring work from his entire career. An extract from a piece I had written for *Ibiza Now* describing *Head of the Goddess* was included in the chronology at the back of the catalogue.

Barry asked me if I would accompany his mother Monica to the show. She was in her eighties, a formidable matriarch who took no nonsense from anybody, including her son. She could match us scotch for scotch in the drinking stakes and distilled a home-produced sloe gin that was pure rocket fuel and sent you off to explore the cosmos. She smoked like a trooper, as did I at the time, and we would sit in a fug of smoke in the green-carpeted studio flat in Santa Eulalia, swapping stories about our families, which connected with Liverpool and the theatre on both sides. Monica had been in the chorus line as a mermaid in 'Water Extravaganza', a touring show managed by Barry's father Bill: one of the tour venues was the Hackney Empire, where Monica swam onstage in a tank. In 2003 Barry would support the campaign to prevent the famous theatre going into receivership, led by the Empire's artistic director, Roland Muldoon, who first met Barry in a dole queue. Monica and Bill also ran the Blue Post public house in Soho, which furnished another rich seam of anecdote.

The Madrid show was everything the Ibiza one was not – uptown, upmarket and up to date. A comprehensive selection of Barry's work was on display, taking in the early work in sand, felt and jute cloth, such as *heap 4* (1967-8), *line 1* (1967-8), and *pile 2* (1967-8), to the most recent hares. There were other animals in the menagerie: elephants, unicorns and horses. Especially striking were

'Barry Flanagan –
New Work',
Fischbach Gallery,
New York, 1969,
private view card

two centaur-like figures, *Sketch on a theme 1 & 2* he had executed in
1987. I saw in them a new direction and told him so when he was
again complaining about the want of fresh ideas. One of the figures
has what looks like a snake for a tail, and I said they were sensual,
which he amended to 'sexual'. He added that such work comes from
another place, and it occurred to me that even heterodox tradition
did not accommodate his type of leap. He reminded me to be wary
of the storms.

There were numerous other testaments to his eloquence both
with form and words such as *if marble smell of spring* (1978), rippling
folds of white marble that tapered to a point, and *Soprano* (1981),
a bronze bird pierced by a gilded arrow, with its beak open in the
act of emitting its death note. Some commentators have seen this as
another example of Barry's humour but it seems instead a product
of profound grief. There is a sense of collision about the piece, as in
Gaudier-Brzeska's *Bird Swallowing Fish* (1914), but in Barry's case there
is an extra element: the unheard spine-tingling cry the bird is making.

*Soprano* was cast in 1981 shortly after *Vessel (In Memoriam)* (1981), a work in bronze with gold leaf also on display. This depicts a boat with no bottom but which instead descends like a jagged shaft to a rope-strewn mound of rock at the sea's base. Along with several other competitors, Barry's eldest brother Mike had been lost at sea during the horrendous storm that hit the *Observer* Transatlantic Single-Handed Race in 1976. His yacht was called *Galloping Gael*. Monica once told me you could get over anything. It was to Mike's loss I think she was referring. The sea, indeed, had a hole in it.

With typical generosity, Barry had flown several people in from Ibiza as well as the entire staff of the London foundry. The latter was back on its commercial feet, as most definitely was its main client. Just as the show recapped his career, so the guest list spanned his life, and his first wife Sue, mother of Flan and Tara, had been invited. At the lunch held the day after the opening, Barry plonked me down next to her. She was an attractive woman with freckled skin and fair hair and was living in Italy with her new partner. By all accounts, she had been expert at accommodating Barry's singular relationship with time and space, providing him and his drinking buddies with hot soup when they rolled up in the early hours to their NW1 house. Somewhere along the line, however, things went wrong, the exact whys and wherefores and who exactly left who a matter of dispute. This coincided more or less with the first flush of Barry's celebrity. I had wondered if there was a connection, inventing in my overheated imagination a Faustian pact whereby the artist exchanged domestic happiness for fame.

It would have been prying to ask Sue about this. Instead, we spoke about Camden, which we both knew well. Then, because you could not stay off the subject for very long, especially with wives and mistresses, we got on to Barry. I described how incredible I found it that the 1960s iconoclast had proved capable of making such figurative and quasi-traditional works as the hares and horses. Sue was also a fan and had donated some of her former husband's prints to the Tate. She had reservations however. One, in particular, stood out: the question of authorship.

When he met new people, Barry would sometimes introduce himself as a sculptor and then raise his hands to reveal palms and fingers without a single mark or scratch on them. It was a sort of party piece but made a serious point. In ten minutes he could produce a sketch that would take others much longer to cast in bronze or carve in marble. The work was his, however, even if he had not personally laid a hand on it. Sue thought this remote manner of authorship impaired authenticity and there was a continuing debate about this. High Victorian sculpture had been made in the Flanagan mode, but Epstein had followed Brancusi in carving the work himself, a tradition continued in part by Henry Moore. Of Barry's contemporaries, the 'girder-welders', such as Caro and Lynn Chadwick, were also hands-on when it came to execution. Barry, however, was happy to delegate, and often only laid his hands for the first time on a piece when it had been finished. Objections to this style of authorship seem today as relevant as advocating a return to the gold standard, though David Hockney has revived the debate by disparaging Damien Hirst's cheerful and lucrative employment of others to pin butterflies or produce jewelled skulls. When it comes to soiled, messed-up sheets, wine stains and torn Rizla packets, however, one can only suppose that Tracey Emin executes all of these herself.

# 15

AS A RESULT of the retrospective Barry was invited to run a week-long drawing workshop at the Institute of Fine Arts in Madrid. This was to be towards the end of October. He asked me to accompany him, but first he wanted me to go to Barcelona to prepare the ground for a project with the engraver Joan Roma. This, as it turned out, had no connection with the projected book of poems by Colinas. It was a little like what had happened with the birds on the wall. Barry had a way of using things for his own ends, a willingness to commandeer if it served his art.

Joan Roma, a short, olive-skinned man, met me at the airport. As we drove into Barcelona he told me he was Jewish and his father had been born in Algeria. It was a Saturday, but we went immediately to his studio in Pedralbes, a pleasant residential area in the foothills of Tibidabo. I told Joan I had worked in the area in the mid 1970s, teaching English at IESE, a business university owned by Opus Dei (the students had carried rosaries in one hand and calculators in the other). The studio was in a side street. Its sole occupant was a long-haired cat with incredibly large yellow eyes that gazed at us all day while Joan gave me a glimpse of the mysteries of his craft.

OPPOSITE
*Field Day 1*
(known by Ibizans as
*'Kouros Horse'*), 1986,
Bronze, 58 ¹/₄" x 74" x
26" / 148cm x
188cm x 66cm
*Field Day 2*
(known by Ibizans as
*'Kore Horse'*), 1987,
60" x 72 ¹/₁₆" x 22 ¹/₆"
installed at 'La Caixa'
in Madrid

A disciple of Blake, Max Ernst and Rilke, Roma was the maker of highly collectable books. He was a bridge between the bank occupied by the writer on one side and the artist on the other. He had a very close relationship with the Catalan painter Antoni Tàpies, producing etchings for him as well as hunting down books for his library: the latter, he said, was the best in Spain. He described his patron as complicated and I told him Barry could be the same. Joan said it came with the territory and described working with Balthus in Switzerland in 1985, an experience that came over as further adventures in sacred monster territory. In a drawer in his office, Joan added, he kept envelopes filled with Tàpies's hair, which the painter insisted was collected each time he had it cut. (Picasso, who nursed the same superstition, had pioneered this practice.)

Joan showed me a book he had made for Tàpies. It was in A3 format with exquisite binding, and I turned the thick sheets finding crosses, numbers, letters scrawled at random and a sock glued to the page. My father once found a dried-out fried egg used as a bookmark in a library book, but a sock seemed more original – and personal, at least regarding smell. There had been an edition of seventy of the Catalan artist's book, which had sold out. The price had been two and a half million pesetas, which made each book worth something in the region of twelve and a half thousand pounds. I asked about the great man's underpants and indeed use had been made of these as well. Joan showed me other books he had made, some on Japanese paper bound in nineteenth-century English cloth. The only book in the entire place not made by his hands lay on one of the worktops. It was a Spanish edition of John Symonds' life of the magician Aleister Crowley, *The Great Beast*.

I told Joan that Symonds had lived in the same West Hampstead street as my family and in my early teens had given me an inscribed copy of his now-forgotten novel, *Bezel*. Symonds had told me how he used to help Crowley inject heroin into a vein that had not yet collapsed. Symonds claimed to have found the Beast repugnant, and so it was ironical that as executor and then biographer he became the keeper of the flame, which burnt ever brighter after the Beatles put Crowley on the cover of *Sergeant Pepper*. Joan told me he had found some correspondence between Katherine Mansfield and Crowley in Paris. I was surprised at this, as I had always thought of

Mansfield as being of another type of persuasion. She had, after all, died of tuberculosis in a cowshed at Gurdjieff's Institute of Harmonious Development in Fontainebleau.

The weather had changed and it was through rainy midtown streets that Joan drove me to a dilapidated building near the Olympic-refurbished França station. This was where Enrique Juncosa lived. Juncosa came from Mallorca and was descended from Miró. Not that many artists meant a great deal to Barry, but Gaudier-Brzeska was one and Miró most definitely another (Barry had hired a tuxedo to present himself at the latter's Tate retrospective in 1964). Enrique was a poet and also art critic for *El País* and had curated Barry's Madrid retrospective. He was a large man with hair that tended to stick up in all the wrong places and a pleasant, guileless face.

His flat was a many-roomed bohemian treasure trove full of work he had collected. He was close to his fellow Mallorquin, Barceló, and my description of the volumes I had seen that day prompted him to show me a folio-sized book he had made with Miquel called *Libro del Océano* (Book of the Ocean). Miquel had filled it with wonderful watercolours of squid and deep-sea divers. Enrique told me of the difficulties he had had with Barry prior to the Madrid show. Dissatisfied with some of the arrangements, Barry had threatened not to attend his own show. 'I might have to take my children to school,' he had explained. Steps had been taken to soothe him but something still rankled. Barry had turned up at the Madrid gallery the night before the opening. The curator had been working with the Basque designer putting the finishing touches to the show. Barry had been in a weird mood and had taken a hammer to his own works in order to make the 'committee', as he called them, leave. Enrique had found the whole thing quite unfair. Only the security guard could reason with Barry, making him coffee and eventually calming him down.

In turn, I told Enrique that Barry had been acting bizarrely the night before he left Ibiza. This I heard from Marty, the co-proprietor of M&M's, who had observed him, in full manic mode, pacing up and down before the bar's full-length mirrors, ranting to his own reflection. Barry was known to get nervous before shows and we had put this down to stage fright; but was a despot, emerging from the chrysalis of fame and money, enveloping the artist-star? Barry had warned me to be wary of the storms. Was another brewing in Madrid?

Enrique and I went for dinner to a Moroccan restaurant. Two couples joined us – one gay, one not so (or so I assumed). The not so's consisted of a petite woman with a provocative mouth and a man with the craggy face of an ancient Roman, dominated by an aquiline nose and jet-black hair. I assumed him to be a filmmaker: he was in fact a lawyer.

When we left the restaurant, he and his wife took me arm in arm on either side. We walked down a street where two central rows of houses had been demolished leaving a wasteland lined with squat, terraced houses. Later, in a bar called the Borneo, after several vodka and tonics, the 'Roman' proposed I join him at home and engage in, what the others assured me later, would be an energetic bout of S&M with his wife. I passed on this and spent the rest of the night in establishments where you had to pay around a thousand pesetas at the entrance in order to drink fake-brand vodka and stand bedevilled by strobe lights and the insidious, mechanical rhythms of *Bacalao* (cod) that pummelled walls and wits. I never found out why such mind-numbing music was named after a fish.

At nine in the morning we ended up at a bar called the James Dean. There were blonde transvestites with silicon-enhanced breasts and freckled backs, and gays dressed as skinheads, French kissing and passing amyl nitrate to each other in the booths. I thought I had a sure-fire antenna when it came to detecting transsexuals but was given a shock when I was told that an especially voluptuous pair of Brazilians were in fact Vicente and Gilberto. The James Dean seemed a place of rampant sexuality where emotions had been discarded. I left, and in the sharp morning light of unfamiliar streets, off balance through lack of sleep, was shown to the metro by a friendly old man. Barcelona, he told me, has a wonderful system: for 550 pesetas you could take ten rides anywhere in the city.

# 16

ON THE MONDAY afternoon, I took the shuttle to Madrid and arrived at the Hotel Reina Victoria around six: this large, elegant, 1927-built affair in Plaza del Angel was the preferred haunt of bullfighters when they were in town. I was given a suite on the second floor next to Barry's. With its luxurious bathroom and goose-down duvet, it was the most opulent room I had ever stayed in. I was still enjoying it when there was a knock on the door. Barry looked tired but was affable as he introduced me to a young Peruvian artist whom the Institute had hired as his interpreter. This put me out a bit. I was in a curious no-man's land between friendship and employment, and anything that gave the latter sustenance was to be welcomed. On Ibiza, however, Barry had told me he wanted me in Madrid for my language and not my translation skills, so I did not feel especially threatened. Thinking about that word 'language' now, I wonder if Barry knew all along that one day I would write up our adventures.

That night we went out for a Japanese meal. A note was passed to Barry containing some flattering words and a little drawing with the word *rabit* [sic] next to it. This pleased him, but in general he seemed preoccupied and more taciturn than usual. He was also making an effort to control his drinking. There was sake on the table, but he was careful to wash this down with large amounts of mineral water. Though Barry had been one of the founding faculty members of the Anti-University in Shoreditch (offering a course on 'Space') and had taught at St Martin's – where he was noted, unsurprisingly, to prefer individual classes to groups – these had occurred a long time in the past, and the few comments he did make gave me the feeling he was apprehensive about the coming week. He was not used to having the discipline of fixed hours in an allocated setting imposed on him. I sensed the prospect was having a sobering effect he was not particularly enjoying. That at least was my reading, though it may be his preoccupations were entirely other.

This moroseness persisted through breakfast the next morning: he was white-faced and did not say a word. After this we went to the Institute, a dilapidated century-old building not far from La Puerta del Sol, Madrid's main square, consisting of an arts complex with a theatre and a studio. The course, which was to be attended by thirty or so students, was due to begin the next day. Barry wanted to prepare the projector in order to display illustrations from the books he had brought, predominantly works of old masters such as Rembrandt and Michelangelo. The short, red-haired woman who helped us with this told me she was glad I was there, that Barry had seemed lonely.

We had lunch in a nearby Galician restaurant, the same we had eaten in with Monica the night before the show in September. We had crab (the paler variety called *buey de mar*), peas and good Galician-style white bread, washed down with a crisp Viña Sol. We returned to the hotel and made – with the benefit of hindsight, mistakenly – for the bar. I drank brandy from a vast balloon glass and Barry a relatively modest J&B. At six we returned to the Institute where we found another bar. When we left, we discovered yet another drinking establishment, a makeshift affair supported by concrete pillars.

Barry seemed to have opened up, and I was in a state of tipsy ebullience, a bit like in Palma before the fight a year before. We talked of art, in particular the 'failed artist', which seemed a particularly horrible term. Three hares had recently been cast in Paris, and I asked about those. Hitherto, he had used the animal as a thing of beauty, such as the original leaping hare, which had looked wonderful in the

Madrid show with its gilded form on a blue wooden base. Others were a form of disguised autobiography, often mapping his state of mind. An example of this is the jaunty top-hat-wearing hare called *Stage Door Johnny* that adorned The Ivy, the celebrated London restaurant, a witty manifestation of Barry's love of the stage and the theatricality of fine dining. The new hares, however, *Awe, Humility and Justice,* all from 1993, seemed to me to be an uncharacteristic attempt to personify abstract notions. When I did get to see them, they struck me as having something plastic and whimsical about them – they could almost have been parodies. *Humility* was a buck hare who carried a divining rod and had a pronounced erection. This was Barry's riposte to Lord Renfrew, Master of Jesus College, Cambridge, and his assertion that the hares lacked sexuality. Being in an art-school environment seemed to have revived memories of his own student years, and he talked about Tony Caro and Phillip King and others I knew very little about at the time like John Latham.

When we left the bar Barry said he was hungry again. I was not, and at this point should have dropped out and gone back to the hotel. We chose an Argentinian restaurant and ordered two different types of steak, which when they arrived almost completely covered the large wooden platters. Barry must have read my lack of appetite in my face for he asked coldly if he was forcing me to eat. I did my best to look delighted by the food.

'You're a punk,' he said for no apparent reason.

'You know very well I'm an old hippie,' I replied, trying to dam this growing and inexplicable fury.

It was to no avail. Several uncomfortable minutes ensued, in which Barry kept on calling me a punk. The waiters were becoming increasingly alarmed. Doubtless, they assumed we were gay and having a tiff.

'You're just like that woman you live with,' Barry hissed in a sudden change of riff.

I was a little stung by this. 'And you're just like the one you don't,' I replied.

Barry lurched to his feet, banging the table as he did so. This knocked over the carafe we had ordered and red wine flooded across the surface and spilled onto my jeans. I jumped to my feet. Barry and I menaced each other for a moment as though about to brawl. Then

I turned on my heel and marched out of the restaurant. One of the waiters pursued me.

'Please don't go!' he said. 'Your boyfriend will calm down.'

I started to cross the road.

'But what about the bill?' he demanded of my retreating steps.

'My boyfriend will pay,' I said huffily.

I wandered aimlessly along Gran Via for a while. Adrenaline, released by the spat, made everything razor sharp. I needed to think about things and went into a bar. In Madrid *carajillos* come in a normal-sized cup with coffee beans floating on top. The mixture is ignited and some of the brandy burns away. Waiting for the flames to die, I asked the barman how many people there were in the city.

'How many are there in Ibiza?' he asked in turn.

This gave me a shock. I peered at the barman, who looked oddly familiar. He told me he had worked that summer in San Carlos, and remembered me from there. He asked me how the writing was going.

I made my way back to the hotel. After about twenty minutes there was hammering on the door. I opened it to find Barry glaring at me. He was waving an envelope, which he thrust into my hand. 'Let's discuss things,' I said, inviting him in, but he was in no mood to talk and marched back to his suite. I opened the envelope and found it contained a cheque. Where it said 'amount', he had scrawled the number 100,500. We had actually agreed on a hundred and fifty thousand pesetas for the job, but who was I to quibble. There was more banging at the door. I opened it again. 'I can handle chaos on my own,' he said, his voice shaking with fury. Again I invited him in, but he turned on his heels. A few minutes later there was yet another loud rat-tat-tat. 'If I want to be a despot, I'll do it in my own way, thank you very much!' About ten minutes later the telephone rang. I lifted the receiver. 'Jessica Sturgess is on her way from Ibiza,' his tone was vindictive, almost a sneer. 'You're dismissed. I hope you're checking out tomorrow!'

The next morning I called his room. If I was hoping for a reprieve such as I had enjoyed in Palma none was forthcoming. 'I can carry on perfectly well on my own,' he confirmed. He asked me to give him the etching plates, sugar solution and pens he had requested I collect from Joan Roma. I gathered these up and took them to his room. I think he was surprised by my lack of indignation.

I checked out an hour later, glad to leave the overcharged environs of the Reina Victoria. I felt a curious sense of freedom. Here I was in Madrid, with an open ticket back to Ibiza and a cheque. I walked to a more downtown neighbourhood and checked into a *pensione* called the Marcelino. Then I went to the Prado and saw the haunting images of the witches' Sabbath and Saturn devouring one of his sons – the black paintings that Goya in old age painted on the walls of his house. After this I had a *menu del día* in a modest establishment near the museum. While drinking coffee, I took out the cheque. Sure enough the figure stated 100,500 pesetas, but under this, after 'pay the bearer', Barry had written in looped purple ink, 'one thousand five hundred pesetas.' In other words, I had about seven pounds and fifty pence to play with in Madrid, and probably nothing at all, since no bank would ever accept such a cheque.

# 17

NEAR MY DOWNTOWN *pensione* was a banner on the side of a building that read: 'Do my eyes deceive me or does desire? Where there was a theatre now there is only street. Or is the street now theatre? Do my eyes deceive me or does desire?' The answer was yes, at least to the second question. The street was a theatre and the play a sleazy police drama in which squad cars pulled up every few minutes besides knots of junkies or groups of Moroccans. Police would jump out and check the suspects' papers. Whether it was a special crackdown or always like this I never found out.

Amongst my friends on Ibiza were two Filipino sisters whose cousin lived in Madrid. I contacted her and we spent three pleasant days together. We visited the Prado and this time I saw the Velázquez, not the Goya. We took a train to the Escorial monastery, the mausoleum of the Spanish kings with its whispering gallery, where we conversed, giggling as we threw our voices from one end of the chamber to the other. We had dinner in a Japanese restaurant, which was a more modest affair than the one I had tried with Barry on our first night. On the third evening I called Barry at the hotel and explained what had happened with the cheque. The next morning I met him in the foyer of the Reina

Victoria and he wrote me a new one. He was cool and white-faced during our interview and we parted stiffly.

The next time I saw him was about a week later back on Ibiza. He passed me in the street and though we did not speak he flashed at me the old two-fingered love-and-peace sign of the hippies. A few days later he came up and spoke to me in M&M's, affable and vague as ever, and I realized one of his more curious features was an ability to fall out and then reconcile with people as though nothing had happened. Barry even made an oblique reference to our fight in recommending the book *Sacred Monsters* by the Soho chronicler Daniel Farson, with its portraits of Salvador Dalí and Brendan Behan, amongst others — demanding, life-enhancing, leaving chaos in their wake. Barry was too smart and big-hearted to become a despot. His was a singular nature and as long as this and his sense of territory were recognized, things were fine. I retraced the events of that night, wondering if the storm was inevitable or if I could have avoided it. I knew my garrulousness must have bothered him. He was nervous about giving the course. He needed a steady hand, not a drunken sailor. Jessica, who replaced me, told me the week had gone very well and I felt angry with myself for missing out on an opportunity to witness Barry in the role of teacher, to see what made him tick from a new angle and maybe even glimpse his secrets.

The rootlessness I had felt in Madrid did not leave me when on Ibiza. My relationship with Kika was now in a permanent on/off mode. Drinking made her anorexic, which in turn rendered the effects of alcohol more pronounced. Her moods were volatile and her screaming deafened the tourists as they lounged on their sun beds on the other side of the creek. It was fortunate that the Spanish had such a high noise threshold, for my landlord never said anything about it. I even moved out of the house for a while and camped on a neighbour's sofa.

I had my old job back and was teaching kids again. I had completed a new version of my Roman book, and the agent in London, who had rejected my previous draft, liked this and thought he could place it. Then the weeks went by and nothing happened. I complained to Barry and he said, 'How are your telephone skills?' I thought we might be in our job interview mode and talked up my eloquence and IT accomplishments until I realized he meant why had I not phoned the bugger. 'I call my agent when I'm on holiday,' he said.

And that was it – my life was a sort of holiday. I would stand at the gate of my house and watch the sun floating down like a red balloon between the pines. Tourists trekked along the path, returning from the beach at sunset, and I would be grateful that what they had for a fortnight I had twenty-four seven. But then the thought came that Ibiza was a place for being, not doing. Barry was right. It was one thing to base yourself on the island, having achieved and set up a network outside, quite another to expect the island to nourish and endlessly inspire you. I was swimming in glue.

Barry's exhibition in Madrid moved to Nantes in the autumn. He had a show arranged for the following year at the Pace Gallery in New York and was spending a lot of time on the mainland. The Madrid show, as well as contacts like Enrique Juncosa, had opened the doors of the Spanish art scene to him. As usual, he was taciturn about his affairs. 'Did you have a good time in Madrid or was that Barcelona?' the cleaning lady would ask. 'Yes,' he would reply.

I handed in my notice at the school in early February. For a few days I felt good with myself, sure the future would be positive. I visited Barry to tell him of my decision to return to England, taking some books that I would no longer need. One of them was an illustrated work about owls, a not-so-subtle response to his occasional complaining about the lack of new ideas. Leaping owls, Nijinski owls... on reflection, I was not sure it would work. On the table he had a book about Feng Shui. There was also an etching, which he handed to me, the first done by Joan Roma. It was of the birds he had drawn. Joan had reproduced the grey blotchy texture of the wall. I admired it and began to hand it back, but he said it was for me.

'I don't know when you'll get your chance,' he murmured, 'but when you do, take as much as you can.'

'I'm going back,' I reminded him.

Far from applauding my decision he seemed dubious.

'Have you got the balls?' he demanded. 'Have you got the balls?' Realizing that he was raining upon my parade, he adopted a gentler tone. 'What are you going there for?'

Fame, fortune and the love of beautiful women, I wanted to say after Shelley, but thought I should sound a more realistic note.

'There's a Master's in creative writing at East Anglia. It's very well thought of. Ishiguro and McEwan have both done it.'

'Your propensity for hero worship does you no credit,' Barry icily observed.

In the days ahead the full horror of what I was letting myself in for hit me. I was forty-one and had not the foggiest notion of what I would do in England. I tried to backtrack but my Spanish partner refused to reinstate me in the school. The next few weeks felt like a type of death as I began dismantling my life on the island and preparing to say goodbye. In my desperation I went to see Barry. I remembered how dubious he had been about my decision and was sure he would save me.

He took me out to the veranda and sat me down with a whisky. The house was a continual work in progress with men labouring both inside and outside. There was a team of Moroccans who had heard of Barry's reputation and would ransack the skip for fragments of pinch pots and torn-up sketches. A truck from the breaker's yard had recently collected the wrong car in the driveway and an almost-new Renault Four belonging to an English worker had been scrapped. To cap it all, a state-of-the art computer had been mislaid. Barry described the culprit as a 'sop to the industry of others'.

Gesturing towards the workers Barry demanded in an exasperated tone, 'What do I bring here? Money and work!'

To a place where a work permit for a foreigner was expensive and time-consuming to expedite, I thought, and few felt the inclination to seek employment in the first place.

'I'd never take a job from a Spaniard,' I said, and then regretted the glibness of what was a standard joke around Santa Eulalia. Barry, however, grinned hospitably. It seemed a good moment to strike. I told him I thought I had been a bit impetuous in quitting my job. He listened with heavy lidded eyes. This was a score he had heard many times.

'You're not family,' he said at the end, making me feel obscurely hurt. 'And besides...' he made a half-circle with his hand, taking in his domain. 'Here you see my practice – as a tradesman this is all I do.'

Before leaving I took a last look at the wall above the fireplace. There was a new addition: 'True judgement resides in the heart.'

I wondered if he had applied this when judging me.

I saw Barry only one more time before I left, which aptly was on April Fool's Day. It was in M & M's and he described Ibiza as 'This haunted, blessed place.' Then he looked at me, smiled and said, 'End of term.'

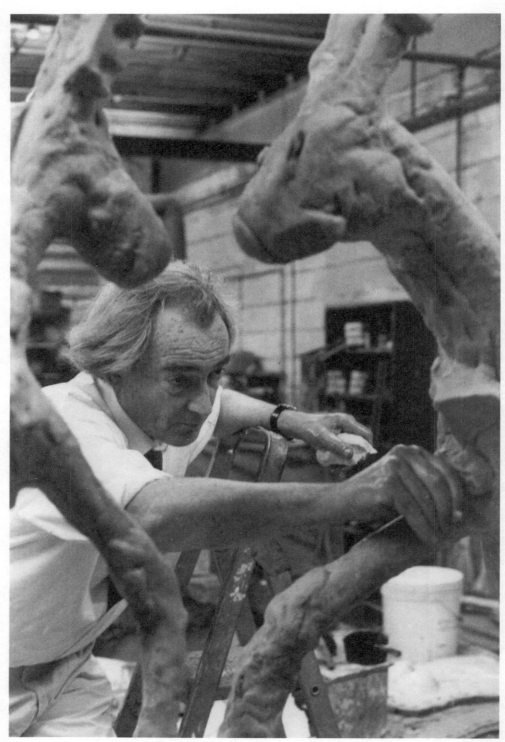

Barry Flanagan working at AB Fine Art Foundry, London, 1998. PHOTOGRAPH Gautier Deblonde

Work in progress in Ibiza, 2006

Work in progress in Ibiza, 2006

Barry Flanagan with hare drawing in Ibiza, 2005

Barry Flanagan with armature in Ibiza, 2005

Barry Flanagan (centre) with foundrymen Jerry Hughes (left) Henry Abercrombie (right), 1998. Photograph credit: Gautier Deblonde

Studio scene with armatures and ceramic pieces

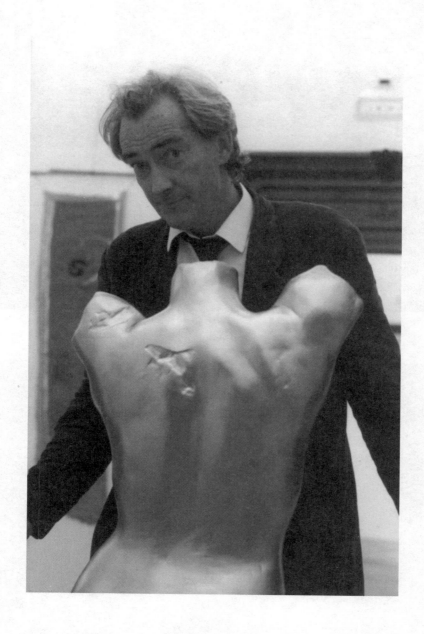

ENGLAND WAS A disaster, but a slowly unfolding one. I stayed with my parents in West Hampstead and worked on a new book through April and May. My mother had been born in Liverpool, into a family of thirteen. My father was also one of many, in his case eight, and had had a disadvantaged upbringing in Wormwood Scrubs and Notting Hill (the latter in those days a very shabby part of London). After serving in the desert in the Eighth Army during the war he had gone into acting. Starting out in repertory theatre, he had then worked in the British film industry in Pinewood and Elstree, and finished up in television. Due to his large build, he had often been typecast as a policeman, appearing as such in *Dixon of Dock Green*, *Z Cars* and as chief peeler in the film *Oliver*. More notoriously, he had been killed by the Daleks in a very early and classic *Doctor Who* and regularly received letters from fans of the series, begging him for signed photos. The fact that he had accidentally dropped William Hartnell, the first Doctor, while carrying him in rehearsal only enhanced his celebrity. My father also wrote a bit, and his play, *The Room They Left*, was shown on television. My mother wrote too, poems and novels, and painted when I was a child. As others are raised to be dentists or tennis players, I was brought up by two people who venerated art, in particular writing, above all things, and were fully supportive of my projects, especially anything literary.

Barry would always pronounce the last word with a ham-actor's stress on the final syllable: li-te-RARY. It was his way of puncturing pretentiousness. Though he accused himself on more than one occasion of neglecting old friends I was a little surprised to find he was still ringing me up. Moreover, he still had jobs for me, including going to discuss with Teresa Gleadowe of the Royal College of Art the possibility of the Tate having *Head of the Goddess*. The Tate already possessed several works by Barry. These included drawings and other pieces donated by his first wife Sue as well as work purchased by them, such as *aaing j gni aa* (1965) – five biomorphic forms made of stitched, dyed hessian filled with plaster and sand whose air of menace and absurdity evokes Jarry (the 'j', in fact, stands for the playwright as well as being the initial of Barry's first name, James). This was the first of Barry's works to attract attention and was exhibited in 1965 in the basement of Better Books. *aaing j gni aa* is a palindrome and Phillip King told me it was he who suggested the white circle that surrounds the figures. Teresa Gleadowe was a close associate of Nicholas Serota, director of the Tate, and would become his second wife in 1997. On 19 May I received a letter from Barry, with his logo of a leaping hare at the top of the sheet. It was typed in capital letters and spaced in such a way that every other line started halfway along the sheet.

MANY THANKS FOR THE PIECE YOU WROTE ON HEAD OF THE GODDESS. AND MANY THANKS FOR PASSING IT TO NICK SEROTA AT THE TATE. I GOT A LETTER FROM HIM SAYING THAT ALTHOUGH THEY HAVE KEY PIECES OF MINE IN THE COLLECTION HE AND LESLIE DON'T NECESSARILY THINK THIS IS ONE OF THEM. THAT HE WAS VERY PLEASED TO RECEIVE THE INFORMATION. I HOPE YOUR BOOK IS GOING WELL AND YOU ENVIGORATE THE PUBLISHER.

Well, I thought, Barry has his rejections too. The Tate's reaction did not surprise me as I thought the work too lyrical for contemporary taste. 'Envigorate' was typical of Barry's dyslexia.

Barry also put me in touch with two friends of his, Alexandra Pringle, who was in publishing, and Tim Hilton, at that time art critic of *The Independent*. They lived with their son near Hampstead Heath. I visited them, but only Tim Hilton was at home. He immediately asked if I were a writer, which made me suspect him of telepathic powers until he explained that Barry was fascinated by writers and was always taking them on. As we continued discussing the sculptor, I got a picture of Barry in his pre-Ibiza days, a well-known figure in The Colony Club, The French House and his 'canteen', Groucho's, hanging out with the likes of George Melly or his peers on the art scene. I mentioned how Barry could go for days without seeming to do any work. Tim Hilton said that was it precisely: he was not a nine-to-five sculptor but someone who worked in bursts. The rest of the time might seem fallow but Barry was in fact creating even when sitting at the bar or staring into space, his mind moving on silence like the long-legged fly upon the stream in Yeats's poem. Barry was full time in the truest sense and this is what made his work so original and alive.

In this period I also visited the foundry where the work was produced. I had been there a couple of times before but on this occasion took Oengus MacNamara with me. Our friendship dated back to our teenage years, when I had attempted to dye Oengus's nearly waist-length hair blue using a washbasin at our place of study, Kingsway College's then full-time annex, in Gower Street, London. Oengus thought blue hair would make a good match for his velvet cloak and leather top hat – he was very much a head of his time. A spell at Drama Centre, and the rigours of life as a jobbing actor, had subsequently instilled a more disciplined approach. Being himself the son of an Irish writer and sculptor, visiting a foundry was highly congenial. His father, Desmond MacNamara, commonly known as Mac, had been one of the leading lights of Baggotonia, Dublin's bohemian quarter of the 1950s, friendly with the likes of Brendan Behan, Patrick Kavanagh, Flann O'Brien and Jack Yeats. J.P. Donleavy based the character MacDoon on him in *The Ginger Man*: 'Small dancing man. It is said his eyes are like the crown jewels.' This also describes Oengus to a tee.

The foundry in Fawe Street in the East End, just beside the Limehouse Cut, occupies a huge square building that was once Spratt's dog-biscuit factory and is a warren of workshops and studio flats used by artists and employees. The workshops are dedicated to different stages of the lost-wax process, so called because the wax that fills the moulds is drained off and replaced by molten bronze. The stages themselves include scaling-up and armature-building, mould-making and sand-casting as well as patination. At any one time, the foundry will be executing work by the likes of Bill Turnbull and Marc Quinn. The foundry also performs repair and you might find the statue of a cricket bowler or the busts of Roman Caesars from Ham House being restored.

In 1969, Ab, the boss, a well-nourished man with a friendly but shrewd disposition, had cast Barry's first bronze, a portrait of Emlyn Lewis, the sculptor's father-in-law and a consultant surgeon. It had been ten years later, in November 1979, that Barry had turned up with a dead hare from the butcher's. At one time 80 per cent of the foundry's work derived from Barry. Though this was eventually to dwindle to 18 per cent the relationship remained a close one. With characteristic generosity, Barry would fly the entire foundry off to all-expenses-paid visits to his shows in Paris, New York, Madrid, Dublin, or, in the case of Amsterdam, for a jaunt to a place where he was not even exhibiting. On one occasion he stuffed notes to the value of ten thousand pounds into Ab's pocket and told him to spend them on the boys.

One of the latter was a Welshman called Mark Jones, a sculptor and maker of original musical instruments in his own right, who went out to Ibiza to work with Barry in the early 1990s. Mark wanted to take photos of the sculptor but felt shy of doing so, until one day Barry invited him to take some. The sculptor had erected a yurt in the garden, which would have made a perfect location. Barry, however, said he would prefer them taken in the wood surrounding the house. They went for a long walk until they came to a glade flooded with sunlight. Barry was holding a Tibetan singing bowl in one hand and asked Mark what was in the other. There was nothing there, but the Welshman said, 'Your imagination.' Mark used up a roll of film but when he came to process it nothing came out due to the excessive light. He had a feeling Barry knew this would happen and the incident was a game or perhaps a lesson.

On a later occasion he had more luck. One morning he found Barry fishing a dead hare out of the pool it had unfortunately fallen

OPPOSITE
Barry Flanagan fishing dead hare from pool in Ibiza, 1994.
PHOTOGRAPH
Mark Jones

into and this time got his photo. Barry is wearing a black kimono and supports himself with a staff as he raises the receptacle in which the deceased animal lies. The sculptor had no squeamishness about dead hares and would eat jugged ones, as he would happily inform those he thought it would shock.

There was to be a show in London in November and when we left the foundry I felt very much out of the swing of things. Barry had seemed more content during my last days on Ibiza, claiming to feel more Mediterranean (Tim Hilton would declare in *The Independent* the following year that Barry's ceramics, on show at Waddington's, could be by a Spanish artist). I wondered, presumptuously, if we had swapped roles. I felt sure my involvement with Barry was over and this joined the other things I was missing: the beach, the sea, and all the heady freedoms of Ibiza. A day or so later this thought recurred in Swiss Cottage Library and glancing at the pile of books on the issuing desk, I noticed one about Feng Shui. It was not the same book I had seen in his house but nevertheless I took it as an omen I would have more to do with Barry. Feng Shui, after all, concerns relationships in space. In 1967 one of Barry's works, *soft shuttered sandwell,* had been placed outside the library. If I had known this then, it would have only bolstered my premonition.

The weeks passed and I grew progressively less comfortable with my situation. Kika, for one thing, was in the house at Niu Blau. I felt responsible for her and for the rent, which, given my current joblessness, would inevitably fall into arrears. It was difficult to adjust to the grey skies, the high price of tobacco, the need to wear socks. Surrounded by gloomy, indifferent faces I longed for the easy camaraderie of Ibiza. I got a job in a West End language school. The work was dull yet demanding, the money poor. The teachers described themselves as 'fruit pickers' because of the ease with which they were hired and fired. I stopped being able to sleep at night. I went to the doctor who seemed intrigued by my predicament and called in his brother, also a doctor. 'This man is haunted by Ibiza,' he said. The only cure for this seemed to be Prozac and Temazepam.

The former gave me aural hallucinations on the tube platform at Tottenham Court Road so I could still hear the song the busker had been playing in the street above; the latter left me more down than ever and exhausted to boot. I could stand it no longer. In high summer, I threw in the job and went to Ibiza. Kika was existing on a diet of vodka and looked fatally thin. A few days after I arrived she was repatriated and put into a clinic to detox. The house was in as terrible a state as its occupant, the furniture broken and demented phrases daubed on the wall in red crayon, a mad parody of Barry's practice. The landlord bought me a drink and asked me to leave. I went back to England, to my 'dark room' as Kika called it. Everything was broken.

My mother said I reminded her of shell-shocked men she had seen in her youth, and it sometimes occurred to me that I had been through a kind of war (an invidious comparison of course to those who really had). With Kika on the one hand, and Barry on the other – both high-maintenance individuals – and all the booze on top, was it any wonder? My psychedelic teens seemed to have finally caught up with me, and the sleepless nights and deadly days seemed like one long bad trip. The worst of it was I was the author of actions I did not understand. I could not fathom any reason for coming back to England, but there was no way back. I forgot how to smile and started having panic attacks. I gazed for long periods at my face in the mirror and it seemed to have assumed the features of a devil. By this time I was seeing a psychiatrist at the Royal Free. I would sit in the waiting room with the other sad, shuffling types, surprised that I had joined them. I explained my predicament to the psychiatrist, but she was not very helpful. She said I looked different from people on the street, more of a Mediterranean type. She could see my point.

In the middle of September, there was a Barceló exhibition at the Whitechapel. I went with Oengus and a painting called *L'Amour Fou* (1985) ('*Mad Love*') spoke to my condition as little else did in that period. In the foreground were the books I had written, the pages drifting out to sea on a tide of indifference. Behind these was the supine red-hued form of a man with an erection. Even the shape of coast and sky resembled that at Niu Blau. The painting seemed to encapsulate all the lust and lunacy I had abandoned and now was so nostalgic for.

Miquel and Enrique were at the exhibition and so was Barry. Looking sleek and fit, the sculptor had just come back from

Salzburg. I introduced him to Oengus and after shaking the actor's hand he turned it over and began examining it. Due to all the work Oengus did in his allotment, the hand was calloused and in places swollen. Barry then showed his hands to Oengus, which the actor said reminded him of a musician's and had not a scratch on them. The sculptor then produced an Irish twenty-punt note, handed it to Oengus and suggested he have a look at it. There seemed no rhyme or reason for this, making you wonder if it were a sort of test, especially as Barry did not seem to want the money back, though Oengus did manage to return it a while later.

After the show the three of us went to Bloom's, a well-known Jewish restaurant in Whitechapel High Street. Unusually for him, Barry ordered a glass of milk with his lamb. Oengus was flabbergasted as this was in total breach of the dairy-with-meat ban in kosher restaurants. (The restaurant, which had been there since 1952, closed down soon after, due to the changing nature of the neighbourhood rather than Barry's dietary howler.) During the meal Barry and Oengus agreed on how much they liked this time of year with the children going back to school. Self-pityingly, I considered how I had no school, no job, no money, no prospect of returning to my spoilt, silly life on Ibiza, as my father called it. The future seemed hopeless. When we said goodbye outside Whitechapel tube station, Barry's parting shot only seemed to rub this in: 'So now it's my island!' he declared.

During the course of the evening, Oengus, unprompted, had told the sculptor I was in a dreadful state and needed help. The phone went a day or so later. It was Barry. There were a few things he wanted me to do for him but my condition and his habitual obliqueness combined to make it impossible for me to understand what these might be. In the end, he grew exasperated: 'Look, I can fire the starter's gun but you have to make it round the course,' he said, making me feel like a racehorse. I was in such a state even scribbling down instructions or dialling a phone number seemed a feat of unimaginable skill but after a few more calls we pieced together something of an arrangement. In exchange for a retainer to cover living costs and expenses I was given certain missions, the first of which commenced with a letter to someone he knew:

Dear J,

Barry Flanagan asked me to contact you in connection with a project concerning pagan Gods. He told me you have some information in this regard particularly related to the God Ti. I was hoping, if you are agreeable, to broaden my knowledge of this deity and any others you might be acquainted with.

Yours sincerely *etc.*

While waiting for word of the God Ti, I was to get hold of and devour a copy of *Stone Mad* by Seamus Murphy, a book celebrating the work of the stone carvers and stonecutters with whom the Irish-born sculptor had trained. Barry himself had first been given a copy in 1976 and it had exerted a profound influence on him. He thought I needed to get 'out and about' and the next part of the commission was to go up to Oxford and investigate the stone heads known as the Philosophers that ring the Sheldonian. I was still having panic attacks and needed someone to hold my hand so I enlisted Oengus for this as well as future projects. Being the son of a sculptor himself, the actor found this quite congenial. Fortunately, he was resting as well as being the owner of an old banger that was comfortable with inclines as long as they were downward … more or less my own condition at this time.

Between 1970 and 1972 a burly, somewhat whimsical sculptor called Michael Black carved the thirteen heads that stand guard over Oxford University's main assembly hall. Each weighing a ton or more, Black's heads were carved in Clipsham stone from the Rutland quarries. Although not a hard stone it is even-textured and weathers excellently. There had been heads outside the Sheldonian since the late seventeen hundreds originally carved by Byrd, which had been replaced by bad Victorian copies. By 1968 these heads had become so disfigured that John Betjeman likened them to 'illustrations for a textbook on skin disease'. Black, who believed the heads had been designed to show different styles of beards, conducted a painstaking search for Byrd's originals and found most of them in Oxfordshire gardens and some in a Hertfordshire cottage. He modelled the new heads on these and hoped at the ceremonial party to have them brought with an escort of Hells Angels from the farm at Binsey where he had carved them. In fact, they were lashed onto a lorry with heavy rope to an accompaniment of Bob Dylan songs and Morris dancing.

Barry's communications, which remained fairly regular through-out this period, were characteristically cryptic to the point of being opaque. Using Oengus as an Enigma machine, I worked out the next port of call was the town of Banbury, near Oxford. While Oengus spent many happy hours in the main library absorbed in his studies of the relationship between Banbury and Oxford, the location of clay deposits and the history of transport in the area, I chain-smoked outside, fending off the giant bats swooping down from the church belfry.

My thought processes were slow in that period, and it took some time for it to dawn on me that far from being random each fresh quest was linked to Barry's life. In 1975, for example, he had left London with Sue and his family. During this period, he worked anonymously as a stonemason at Jocelyn's Yard in Oxford, blocking out one of Black's heads. After this he had a brief apprenticeship to the delightfully named Mr Mold, a dental technician. This was in Banbury where he formed a great affection for the local Hornton stone, which he used liberally during this period. Naturally, Barry did not mention any of this. I had to make it round the course on my own.

Every cipher we cracked seemed to spell one word: stone. Consequently, Oengus and I began an exhaustive tour of quarries. First, we visited Hornton, near Edgehill, where local legend has it that the soil is still red with the blood of cavaliers and roundheads fallen during the battle that took place there. Hornton stone, also known as Ironstone or Gingerbread stone, is hardwearing, noted for its ease of use and can be anything from light brown to blue. Used for many Oxford colleges as well as St Paul's Cathedral, it was a favourite of Henry Moore and Eric Gill. Then we headed to the West Country and the Mendips, visiting Beer, the Ham Hill quarry with its Saxon forts, and Doulting, which provided the stone for Wells Cathedral.

Barry continued baffling us with clues via the phone. It was increasingly apparent that this was not just an abstract quest for stone, but that if we pieced the jigsaw together correctly, we were engaged on a biographical journey. He suggested, for example, we go to Bath and look up Peter Randall-Page. Now a successful sculptor in his own right, Randall-Page had undertaken the work of pointing out in a classical Italian manner Barry's *Enlarged Marble Shape* (1978) for an exhibition at the Serpentine Gallery in 1978. Barry had used a three-ton stock of stone imported from the 'marble supermarket' at Pietrasanta for this. 'Something to cut my teeth on,' he had said at the time.

Unfortunately, Randall-Page was not in the local telephone directory. I could probably have made contact with him through his gallery or dealer but such a feat was beyond my fractured skills. We had a bit more luck at Beer in Devon, however, where Barry asked us to find Fred Newton, formerly an apprentice mason at the local quarry, who had given Barry a job as a beach-hand in 1959. Wherever we went gaffers and museum curators were delighted to share their knowledge, which they did exhaustively. Oengus, by this time, was completely stone mad and on a separate trip, absorbing everything about Purbeck and Portland stone. And me? I was just crazy.

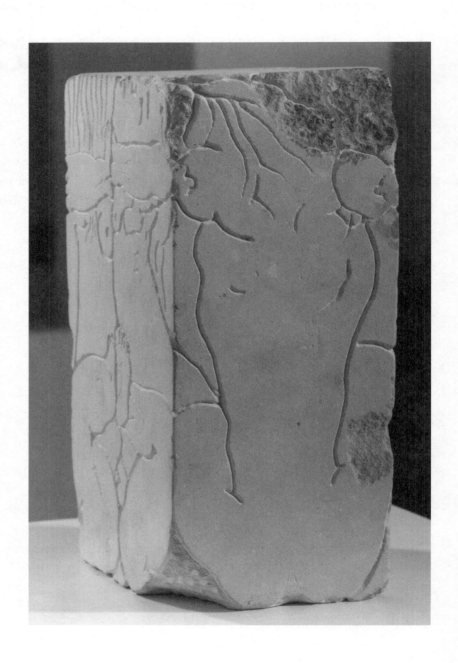

# 19

THE RESULTS OF my investigations with the actor became 'No Stone Unturned', an illustrated document of more than a hundred pages. I had typed this out in upper case, in the belief it facilitated Barry's reading, and gave it to him when we met in Groucho's in early December. We were alone in a private room and along with the report I provided samples of stone from the quarries mentioned in it. He played with these between his fingers for a while, admiring the golden Hamstone, the Doulting stone, with its characteristic lustre, and the greenish-grey Purbeck marble. He greeted the white stone from Beer like an old friend, having employed it in such works of the 1970s as *Tantric Figures*, incising fluid lines into its yielding surfaces. Unusually, Barry did not want to be read to but began reading the piece himself. For obvious reasons, I had given Oengus the new name Seamus and his input was apparent in every line.

OPPOSITE
*Tantric figures*, 1973,
Beerstone and acrylic,
12" x 7 ¹/₂" x 5 ¹/₂" /
33cm x 19.1cm x 14cm

Seamus and I set off on a Wednesday morning whose sunniness is typical of the mildest November since 1659. Four hours later we reach Beer where we check into the comfortable and highly reasonable Dolphin Hotel and admire the collection of Victorian and Edwardian memorabilia displayed upon its walls. After this we stroll down to Beer cove. To the right of the road leading to the harbour, lovely allotments, still verdant in mid November, scale the cliff road. To the left, there is a Belleview of concrete and stone, the better to enjoy the pocket-sized prospect below. This consists of a perfect semi-circle of striated cliff and stepped shingle beach. Large colourfully painted trawlers grace this exquisite indentation on the coast – secluded, private and sufficient.

Hedged by the narrow valley landscape, the village straggles off the one road to the sea, supplemented by the road from Seaton, which curves round the eastern cliff. There are a few hotels, pubs, the 'social', a baker and greengrocer's etc. The Mariner's Hall, open only for events, has a forlorn, deserted air at this autumn's waning. On either side of the main street there is the truckling roar of water swallowed by the open storm drains – a hazard to drunks and errant drivers.

The roads and environs are explored in the gloaming, caves shut, beach open. We retire to The Barrel of Beer where we encounter an importunate drunk who claims to be the author and director of several famous TV productions. A scruffily dressed man with drooping eyelids and a downturned moustache, he explains how his wife, family and most of his friends are dying of cancer. At forty-two he is burnt out, dispossessed of 'two cars, a house with tennis court', ripped off for £175,000 by a dishonest broker, in short bereaved and bankrupt. As Seamus puts it, 'This 'personality' seems to have crash-landed with the force of a medium-sized meteorite. His claim to personal grief leaves anyone else's on the nursery slopes. He has tasted the dizzy heights of Olympus only to be dashed into Tartarus. McNeff is completely outclassed.'

The next morning I awake to a peace that is very welcome after London. The gulls wheeling outside, hailing each other beneath a periwinkle sky, enhance this. After poached eggs on toast and some of Seamus's Algerian coffee, which the proprietor hospitably brews for us, we take another gander at the cove,

*Tantric goddess,
1973, Beerstone and
painted with acrylic,
6" x 14" x 8" / 15.2cm
x 35.6cm x 20.3cm*

where sunlight bounces off waves and sparkles on wet shingle. All the fishing boats we admired the day before are out to sea, but the fish shop is open offering freshly caught crab, cod and mackerel. The owner turns out to be Roy Newton, who must bear some relation to Fred. I ask him to trawl his memory for Barry Flanagan. I supply a description, but still the nets of memory hold no catch. A few minutes later, however, he calls me back. 'Didn't his mother rum [*sic*] the Lobster Pot?' he says. Well, did she?

After this Seamus and I go up to the quarry. The caves, famous for the Roman workings that cover their surfaces like the letters of a language as indecipherable as Etruscan, closed at the end of October, but the quarry opposite is open. We enter the work's office located a hundred yards or so from the entrance. 'Is there anyone here?' I ask. 'No,' a voice announces from an adjacent room.

Telling me he would finish it later, Barry put the document down. We were both pleased. He, because I seemed to have been restored to myself and I because something tangible had indeed come out his help – it had not just been charity. We left Groucho's and went to another private members' club further up Dean Street called Black's. We had dinner with a film director Barry knew, during which I thought I was back on Ibiza and drank too much. Then we went to The Colony Club, with its emerald green walls and famous stool next to the bar, from which the proprietor Ian Board was wont to rain caustic comments on his clientele. There was a taboo in place against anybody else sitting on the stool, which did not deter me as I slumped onto it, shocking the regulars. I then used it as a launching pad to my next port of call – the floor. Barry and the director had to heave me up and carry me out to the street. When they were sure I was okay, they put me on the tube home. The acute sense of exile I felt from Ibiza was driving me mad. During a disturbed night, I got up and fumbling about in the dark knocked one of Barry's pinch pots off the mantelpiece. The next morning I found the broken shards of baked clay on the floor. They seemed an apt mirror of my state.

Barry once told me that he liked to have a stake in anything he was connected with; geographically this meant flats and houses, of which he had several. Some were rented, some were owned, and during the time I knew him were variously in Dublin, London, Amsterdam, Paris and New York. On Ibiza alone he had the house off the San Carlos Road; another in the country towards San Miguel that became Renate's; a studio flat in Santa Eulalia; and for a time, a flat in Figueretas, a not-so-salubrious quarter of Ibiza town. Sometimes people read too much into this. There was a rumour rife amongst the Spanish on the island that the sculptor kept two different houses for two different women according to Antonio Colinas in his memoir of Ibiza, *Los Días en la Isla* (*Days on the Island*), which contains a chapter on his friendship with Barry. Legend also apparently attributed ownership of a hotel in Goa to the sculptor, something he never mentioned to me.

A few days after the debacle in Dean Street, I got a call from Barry inviting me to Barcelona. I found him in a flat in the centre of the city, typically fitted out with wall-to-wall green carpeting. I had brought a bottle of duty-free Johnnie Walker and we had a convivial time that stretched into the early hours. Barry seemed relaxed and cheerful: the demons were in retreat. Recently, he had taken to speaking to me in a more direct way, and there were fewer riddles or turns of speech. He talked about his career and seemed to find his own success a matter of wonder, admitting with a slightly roguish smile that there had been an occasional element of sleight-of-hand in his creations as well as a bit of playacting to his celebrated eccentricity.

Barcelona seemed totally transformed from the glum city I had known in the year of Franco's death. There was a magical night with a man on a white stallion and circus performers at the Fundació Joan Miró, which we went to with Enrique and Barry's daughter Tara, who was also in town. We visited a catering school and had a specially prepared meal, which began with Manhattans and ended with fine brandy (there was some food as well). We visited Joan Roma's studio and Barry gave me number two copies of each of the series of etchings made for him, literally hot off the press. Mainly in muted greys and beige, these consisted of hares, leaping, dancing and a Nijinski. There was an unusual one bound in white wrapping like an Egyptian mummy with the number five circled in a thinking bubble coming out of its head [see *Trans fixed*, 1994, page 49]. I would find out later there was a hare god, with similar bindings, in the Egyptian pantheon. The work may reference his relationship with his mother Monica, which was a warm one but had its feistier moments. Indeed, as he would remark a few years later, Monica spent the last five years of her life with him on Ibiza, while he, due to the war, had had her exclusively to himself for the first five of his. The series was to be marketed by Tàpies's nephew. Considering all I had done was set things up with Joan Roma in the vaguest of ways one Saturday, my reward was very generous.

We also visited an exhibition at the Fundació Antoni Tàpies called *The Spirit of Fluxus*, devoted to the informal grouping of artists in the 1960s that traversed several disciplines and embraced concrete poetry, happenings and installations. In music, John Cage was its most famous exponent, in art, Yoko Ono. Barry had driven Ono and her husband, the filmmaker Tony Cox, round London in September 1966, acting like an unofficial roadie. This was the time of the Destruction in Art Symposium at the Africa Centre, Convent Garden, in which they all participated. Yoko Ono had performed *Cut Piece*, where she let members of the audience cut her clothes off with a pair of scissors.

There was a film at the Barcelona show of her doing this. Barry had collected dresses from Biba for her to use and on one occasion had accompanied the piece by riding slowly round the room on a white racing bike with drop handlebars, his shoulder leaning against the wall. Typically, he made no mention of this as we watched the film together. Yoko Ono's destruction of dresses was relatively tame, however, compared with John Latham's penchant for public book burning or Ralph Ortiz's decapitation of a chicken, for which he and others were prosecuted. The most celebrated consequence of the destruction symposium was to inspire one attendee, a former art student called Pete Townsend, to instigate The Who's practice of smashing up equipment at the end of shows.

Barry disliked formal intellectualizing, and despite being better placed than most to comment, continued to say little as we toured the exhibits. There were cabinets full of oddly juxtaposed objects such as matchboxes and cards; a photo of a woman drawing a bow across a man's back as though playing the cello; a plate with a half-eaten sandwich on it. There was a playfulness and relish for absurdity that made it easy to draw a parallel with Barry's work. Like his younger self the movement was going in every direction: Fluxstamps, Fluxfilms, Fluxorchestra *etc*.

We paused before a photo of Joseph Beuys. The German artist, wearing his trademark felt hat, was at the Festum Fluxorum in Dusseldorf performing the first movement of his Siberian Symphony on the piano. There was a chalkboard to one side of him with a dead hare hanging from it. Beuys's most famous piece of performance art was in fact called *How to Explain Pictures to a Dead Hare* (1965) in which, his head covered by honey and gold leaf, the artist spent three hours cradling the dead animal in his arms as he talked about the great masters in tender whispers. This gives rise to the intriguing conjecture that Barry's most commercially successful creation, the frequently gilded hare, might in fact pay homage to one of the more subversive moments in twentieth-century art – such allusions being very much in the spirit of the sculptor's practice. It was probably more than coincidence that Beuys and Barry, shamans and mavericks both, occupied adjoining rooms at Tate Modern in its early days.

# 20

IN BARCELONA I sometimes wondered if I was still on the payroll, and in fact it turned out I was not. I had no cause to complain. Barry had been more than generous. I had eventually managed to finish my novel, a work of comic fiction with supernatural overtones. In the new year I found work at a language school in Hendon, which despite poor pay was a congenial establishment. I was back on some kind of track.

In February I heard there was to be a gathering of 'old muckers' in Willesden. The venue was a mock-Tudor semi-detached house crammed full of people I had known in my teens. I was in the sitting room when two young girls rushed in. One had long hair and round John Lennon glasses. She seemed oddly familiar, though I could not place her. Something impelled me to talk to her but her companion, who had a snub-nosed freckled face and wavy chestnut hair, said, 'My sister's deaf,' and the pair of them ran off giggling. I followed them into the kitchen, where they stopped to speak to a short woman who was spreading Brie onto a baguette. Then they ran off into the garden. The woman was also familiar. This was because of a one-night stand in 1979. I remembered this vividly as a couple of months after she had called to tell me she was pregnant. She was not certain if I was the father so I suggested we wait for the birth. I had heard no more about it until this moment. I went up to the woman and said, 'I think we should talk!' This had a slightly comical effect. The recipient of this information gave me a wide-eyed stare, the Brie-smeared baguette now suspended in space. 'You're not Richard?' she demanded.

I went round to the woman's spacious garden flat about ten days later. She explained that she had not been in touch because she thought someone else was the father. Apart from the eldest, who might be mine, she also had two other daughters, the ten-year old who had been at the party, and a five-year-old. The younger sisters' dad, whom the mother had been estranged from for several years, was the other contender in the fatherhood stakes. This began an interesting game of whether the deaf girl was mine or not that lasted for well over a year. I visited as frequently as possible, fascinated by the notion that I had a daughter.

Our ears were identical, which to the mother was conclusive of my paternity. Astara, as I was pleased the deaf girl had been named, could also cup her hands together and make farting noises, a teaching tool I had employed for years to indicate mistakes to Spanish children. I knew from the hundreds who had tried and failed to imitate me that this was a rare (for want of a better word) accomplishment. Astara's skin was like mine: olive, easily tanned, plagued by spots in adolescence. Her eyes were a similar shade of green to my own. Indeed, I found an old photo of myself at fourteen with long hair, round glasses and the same dreamy expression. I looked like her twin. Her teeth were jumbled, however, but in this they were like my mother's. Her nose was different, straighter and more pronounced, and it was to take some time before I discovered where this shape came from.

Apart from the occasional intelligible word, Astara's speech was incomprehensible but had none of the nasal quality that can mark the profoundly deaf. Her voice was mellifluous and she laughed naturally and long. She seemed amused by the situation and was remarkably free of self-pity. The only time she referred to her deafness was to tell me she was sorry I might have ended up with a disabled child. Though she had made her own mind up that she had a different father from her sisters a while before my appearance, she was not sure if this was me. I began to learn a little sign language and to fingerspell but writing was our main means of communication. Apart from jumbled syntax and endearing spelling errors such as 'primrose' instead of 'promise', hers was not so bad. Communication was a challenge but on occasion I suspected she was way ahead of the game. Getting her to go to bed was always a problem especially one night when she wanted to stay up to see the Indoor Bowls Championship on TV. I did not have a clue why such a pursuit should interest her until she made a little mime that made it obvious she thought 'bowls' meant 'bowels'.

Signs and resemblances accrued. She liked painting and did so in a vivid style almost exactly like my mother's and my own when I had experimented with the medium in my teens. My parents were fastidious about cleanliness. Astara and I, however, were messy and bohemian. Sometimes the correspondence in our natures was such it made me wonder if traits were not transmitted over Darwinian epochs but within a generation – a new model of evolution that is gaining ground today. It had long been a joke in my family to snatch a newspaper from somebody else when we had finished our own. We liked reading at mealtimes and the first occasion Astara and I had dinner at my parents' flat she grabbed *The Evening Standard* clean out of my hands.

My father, however, poured rain on the notion that I had stumbled on his long-lost grandchild. Astara also remained sceptical. It was an unsatisfactory situation and I began to investigate DNA testing, which at the time was expensive and required a long wait for the results. Every so often Barry phoned and in June 1996 he invited me down to Ibiza. He seemed as focused as he had been in Barcelona and when we discussed my 'find' told me something like that could not be left in doubt. He was donating *Head of the Goddess* to the museum and a ceremony was held in the ground floor gallery with Elena and some local dignitaries present. Colinas read the poem in Spanish and then I did the same in English.

After the ceremony Barry, Renate, Alfred, Annabelle and I had dinner outside at a restaurant near the museum. Then I went off with Barry. We drove towards Santa Eulalia and drew up outside a large pink building besides the turn off to the village of Jesús. Permissiveness was becoming ever more rampant on the island, with strip clubs springing up daily. The pink building was a brothel. We made to go in but a bouncer at the entrance told us it was full. We went instead to Can Bufi, a bar on the Es Canar road that had been a gay hotel and was now used to raise funds for an HIV charity run by Suzy Elliott, widow of the actor Denholm. Barry chatted with her for a while.

When I got back to London, we did the test. First the mother's, then Astara's and finally my own blood was analyzed. After three weeks the results came through: the probability of my being the father was 98.4 per cent. This was very high but not conclusive. I realized that had we done the same test when Astara was first born, we would never have been sure. Advances in biological science delivered me a daughter, for three weeks later the DNA results came back as 99.9 per cent conclusive – there is always a 0.1 per cent margin of error.

When I told my father, he disappeared for a little while and came back with a faded photograph of his brother Tommy, who was killed in the war and is buried in Arnhem. There in profile was Astara's straight nose and slightly crooked smile. My daughter herself took more convincing but came round eventually.

Astara was attending a special needs school in South London. The school was doing its best but not really catering for the clear talent she had shown for painting and sculpture, areas in which she could of course operate at no disadvantage. She also disliked the travelling and had a fit in my presence that resulted in her going to hospital for three days. Tests detected no trace of epilepsy and as the seizure had been induced by stress we decided to pull her out of school and send her to a fine arts college in Belsize Park. She flourished in this environment and did very well in her art GCSE. The college was private and fee-paying, however, and there was no state funding available. Astara's grandmother managed to raise some money from her former employer, the BBC, but it was not enough to cover the course and it looked as though we would have to pull her out at the end of the autumn term of 1996. Her tutors thought highly of her and this seemed a great shame. After some deliberation, I wrote to Barry, asking him if he would be prepared to help towards sponsoring my daughter, either by the donation of money or a work.

About a week later I found a letter in the hallway. It had been sent from Dublin and consisted of a large sheet of paper with the

Richard

&

Long a moving
Line

yrs

Barry

Nov 12/96

Dublin

Letter, 1996

familiar logo of the leaping hare at its head. Apart from the date and Barry's signature, the only words were 'Richard or Long a Moving Line', written in reddish-brown ink. The phrase haunted me. Here were ripples! Here were hues! On one level it could be interpreted to mean that my words had moved him but on another that Astara was my line, as in family line, and he was wishing us well. It made me wonder if the multifaceted nature of such language was deliberate or accidental — if Barry himself was always aware of what he was doing. There is a drawing he made in 1979 called *Keeping ones own tracts open*, which consists of that phrase written in lower case on the bottom of a blank sheet of paper with the words in upper case repeated in mirror writing above it. Barry's dyslexia did at times produce some interesting, not to say bizarre, results but 'tracts' was not one of them. The sculptor was very much keeping his 'tracks' open and wittily underlining this by using a near homophone — one that defines the most dogmatic and restricted of forms.

The upshot of our communication was that Barry picked up a large part of the tab for my daughter's studies. Moreover, he informed the college that if for any reason she dropped out he would like the money to be used for someone else.

# 21

**EVERY SO OFTEN** Barry would call for a friendly if still at times bewildering chat. He rarely mentioned business and it was via newspapers or from others I heard about the giant hares lining the streets of Park Avenue in New York, the exhibition focused on 'pataphysics in France, or the exhibition at Waddington's in Cork Street, which highlighted the relationship between his drawing and sculpture, called, with typical wordplay, Seeing Round Corners. On a more personal note, I heard that he had left Ibiza and after a spell in Amsterdam had settled in Dublin. His leaving the island did not surprise me. The endless leeching of prospective handmaidens must have become very wearisome. Almost supernaturally generous, he could still complain about how fast the wad of notes in his inside pocket was shrinking. Moreover, his pale skin did not tan easily and the intense heat of the summer put him out of sorts.

During this time I researched and wrote a book that grew out of the story that had been published in *Rapid Eye* without my knowledge. *Sybarite Among the Shadows* is a factional narrative set in 1936 with a 'li-te-RARY' dimension. It follows a day in the life of the minor poet Victor Neuburg, which begins with a visit from his protégé, Dylan Thomas, and ends spectacularly with magical rituals conducted with his former master, Aleister Crowley, on the banks of the Thames. In between there is the opening of the Surrealist Exhibition, encounters in the bohemian fleshpots of Soho and Fitzrovia with the likes of Augustus John, Wyndham Lewis and Nina Hamnett, and a plot to avert the abdication of Edward VIII. The book was difficult to place but after the usual avalanche of rejections it found a home with Mandrake of Oxford, an independent publisher that specializes in the occult. The launch took place at my workplace, the London School of English in Holland Park, in November 2004 and the help of colleagues was greatly appreciated. Guests included Snoo Wilson, the playwright, and the late Brian Barritt, who with his mentor, the LSD guru Timothy Leary, had replicated Crowley and Victor Neuburg's psychedelic workings in the Algerian desert (rites themselves based on the Enochian Calls made to the angels by John Dee, the Elizabethan magus, and Edward Kelley). I invited Barry but at the last moment he could not make it, so I sent him a copy. I inscribed this to '*il miglior fabbro*', that is 'the better maker'. This was the quote from Dante that Eliot used when he dedicated *The Wasteland* to Ezra Pound. It may sound pretentious, but I meant it.

In early December Barry rang to say how much he was enjoying the book. This both pleased and surprised me. The former because Barry rarely expressed his opinions in such a straightforward manner; the latter because as we almost never discussed books or art in the accepted sense. I was still labouring under the delusion that he was not a reader, when he was in fact an avid one. A few days later he rang to say he had finished the book and was highly enthusiastic about it. But how was I going to get it across, he kept saying – a good question, as neither I nor Mandrake had great marketing resources at our disposal and without them, sadly, many books get lost. He invited me down to Ibiza where he had bought the house on the San Carlos Road back from the man he had sold it to – Yuppie Richard, whom many people confused with me. I was already booked to go to Thailand. Then the tsunami happened. I cancelled my ticket and a few days after Christmas flew down to Ibiza.

The house had changed considerably since the last time I had seen it. The wall around it had been rebuilt and an electronic gate installed so any cars were only admitted at the discretion of the owner. The house and grounds were in an orderly state, with a round swimming pool in the garden, and a well-furnished interior with comfortable rooms and the inevitable green carpeting everywhere. The place had gone from squat to residence. Indeed, that sense of transformation from something makeshift and hippie to a more conventional environment was my main impression of the island itself over the next couple of weeks. One by one, the wild things and drunken artists who assailed you in the Kiosko had been expelled – Kika, Mike Shaw, Crazy Jane, Bo – and a more sanitized reality installed. Excess was zoned to San Antonio or parts of Ibiza town and exported like a brand in the ancillary form of fashion and music such as Café del Mar. The number of residents on the island had doubled in a few years. Judging by the luxurious yachts in the marina and designer brands that filled the shops, it was easy to assume most of the newcomers were rich.

Barry was still resident in Ireland with a house in one of the most upmarket neighbourhoods in Dublin but Ibiza had got under his skin, as it did to most of us, and this partially explained his return. Also, he was now with someone who was practically a local girl. Jessica Sturgess was English, from a cultured diplomatic background, and had travelled widely as a child. She had then spent many years in Goa when it, like Ibiza, was still pristine and not a tourist hotspot. After this she had moved to the White Island. Tall and willowy, she spoke excellent Spanish and was a great ally to Barry in every sense.

I stayed with them for just under three weeks. Given the length, I had been a little nervous about overstaying my welcome, but all went well. Barry now sported a pointed greying beard, which gave him the look of a benevolent wizard. He usually wore a black hat and gave me one too, which made me feel I was finally an artist. We celebrated New Year at a well-known restaurant called Daffer's in Santa Eulalia. Barry danced in his jerky way, completely at home with the expat crowd. We also went out for dinner on his birthday on January 11. Most of the time, however, we spent in the house or on the veranda, the weather being sunny and warm almost without exception.

Barry would potter about and tinker with a clay statue of a woman with a bowl-like shape on her head and features that struck me as a cross between Jessica's and Annabelle's. In conversation the sculptor would vaguely refer to a foundation he was thinking of establishing on the island, perhaps as a home for the work of local artists. He would mention J.P. Donleavy, the American author who lived in Ireland and had recently become a friend. We would speak fondly as well of absent friends such as Foxy, who had died in 2002. An obituary in the *Daily Telegraph* highlighted her penchant for taking her clothes off if she felt she was receiving insufficient attention. I had, in fact, witnessed her open her sarong when hitchhiking, and many an Ibicenco lorry driver had been astounded by a flash of her plump and dusky torso. Barry would also talk about John Latham, who, at the grand old age of eighty-three, would once more become a figure of controversy later that year. Latham was to have an exhibition at the Tate, but due to the London bombings of 7 July the gallery withdrew his *God is Great* – torn copies of the Bible, the Talmud and the Qur'an embedded in a six-foot-high sheet of plate glass. When Latham died in January 2006, Damien Hirst remarked: 'He proves it is possible to be an *enfant terrible* for ever.'

One evening Barry showed me his erotic drawings, some of which he had done on a palm top. There were two figures whose penises were supported by string so that one was raised and one drooped. Another showed a man cupping the breasts of a woman he was standing behind. The man had a prominent moustache. I said he looked like Lord Kitchener, but Barry told me he was supposed to be Salvador Dalí. There was a work with the title *Seranade* consisting of three nudes and a man playing the piano. A drawing of a dragon sucking on the stem of a penis had lightning forking off the latter to represent, I assumed, the tingling of the nerve ends. It seemed Barry was playing with the idea of the dragon as a symbol – it was certainly a more sexual one than the hare.

The 'hedge-springer' was not entirely forgotten, however. One evening I shared with Barry an etymological nugget I had recently heard, that the word 'news' apparently derived from north, east, west and south. This had a winning logic to it and neatly explained why the uncountable noun ends with an 's'. It is also, in all likelihood, complete rubbish. Notwithstanding, in the following year Barry was to make a new sculpture consisting of four Nijinski hares mounted one on top of the other, each facing one of the cardinal points. He called this *News* (2006).

Barry had said he wanted to draw me, and on my last evening we went to my room in the north wing of the house. I sat on the armchair. Barry squatted down on a large cushion on the floor near me. Jessica crouched on the green carpet. There was an air of ritual.

Barry asked me to read out loud from a book, much of which I had read to him that week, Virginia Nicholson's *Among the Bohemians*, an amusingly anecdotal account of artists and people in love with the lifestyle. Barry had enjoyed the stories greatly but admitted to a sense of unease with what had become an all-too-obvious cliché – his emphasis on trade had been to demystify the process: a way to release the artist from a cloying, distracting aura. He said he found something disquieting about it all.

While I read from Chapter Four, 'Dwelling with Beauty', which deals with bohemian décor, he started making rapid incisions on a dry point engraving plate. I did not look at him but gleaned from the scratching sounds that he was working with great swiftness and concentration. After a few lines I came upon the pleasing synchronicity of 'the distractingly handsome artist sketching at the next table', which made us all laugh. It was over after I had read about a page and a half. Barry thought he had finished but after a brief scrutiny went back to it as there was something not right with the nose. With that done we looked at the finished product. The portrait was not flattering. I had been given a large nose and chin and seemed to have two faces, one gazing down (presumably at the book) and one looking ahead. This gave me two ears on the same side of my face and two pairs of glasses. I asked Barry about the glasses and he said the second pair was a shadow and added, 'An element of caricature often intrudes.' 'Caricature' was a word he had asked me to spell the previous day.

The next morning he asked me to read from *Among the Bohemians* again. He was very serious and seemed intent on finding something. This turned out to be 'in the timeless Bohemian heartland' on page one hundred. He copied this down carefully. Then he asked what I wanted from 2005. I said I hoped my book would find a readership. When I asked the same, he said he was tired of moving about and wanted to settle down.

Back in London I wrote a poem called 'Portrait', which I sent him. Towards the end there was a line that said, 'The self in its grinning jar as the tide rolls out.' A couple of weeks later I received a letter from Ibiza. In lower case, written in dark ink in Barry's sloping hand, was the following:

> *The portrait of you I will print in 2 versions one of which will be reduced from the life size one and that print will be put in a storage jar. I hope the thought pleases you.*

Reflecting on this, I wondered if Jarry once more had got into the works. The Frenchman, after all, was a great enthusiast for reduction. He lived in a tiny room that his space-saving landlord had erected between the third and fourth floors of the house. Jarry's bed was a reduction of a bed, being a pallet, and he used a reduction of a table, as the bed was the only item of furniture in the room. In other words, he penned his plays and articles while lying flat on his stomach on the floor beneath a reduction of a portrait of him by Rousseau, most of which he had burned away to leave only the head. The letter continued:

> *We, friends on one hand, should suggest that you contribute in future on an advanced return to a course devoted entirely to you. One long weekend. Your career we cheer, and as you may guess, there is nothing short of devotion in good heart*
> *Bon favoro*

I was baffled by the reference to the course devoted entirely to myself, unless it was a dig about the one I had flunked in Madrid. The postscript, however, was far clearer. Anyone reading my poem would have gleaned that its author was a bit lonely and Barry had added, 'You may release yourself from solitary by dispensation from within.'

# 22

IN JUNE 2006 Barry had a major retrospective at the Irish Museum of Modern Art in Dublin. The entire foundry as well as friends, family and associates from England, France, Hungary and Spain were put up in The Morrison Hotel on the banks of the Liffey. There were flowers and a bottle of champagne in every room as well as someone on hand who would pay for any extra drinks or food you might want to order. Giant hares leapt, drummed and boxed along O'Connell Street and there was a ceremony at The Hugh Lane Gallery (home to the disorder of Francis Bacon's relocated studio) at midday. A few hours later, after a performance by a youth orchestra in the grounds, J.P. Donleavy opened the exhibition at IMMA with an abrasive speech entitled 'Lobbing Hand Grenades', which consisted of fulsome praise for Barry, an attack on the powers that be, and a hailing of the new Irishman: the Protestant-Catholic.

As in Madrid in 1993, the exhibition spanned Barry's entire career with the addition of two curious woodcarvings of medieval bishops, placed in the museum's garden, which he had 'found' in Holland. Later, there was a violin recital, and the next day an entire

OPPOSITE
*Thinker on Rock,*
1997, bronze, edition
of five plus three AC
144 ¹/₈" x 73 ¹/₄" x
103 ⁹/₁₆" / 366.1cm x
186.1cm x 263cm

restaurant was commandeered for a party with a jazz band. Barry had declared he was retiring, but nobody believed him.

At Dublin airport when leaving I found amongst the cards describing Irish family names one about Flanagan. The coat of arms consists of an oak tree on a green mound beneath a knight's helmet. The name itself derives from the Gaelic Flann meaning 'red' or 'ruddy' and was originally written O'Flannagain. The O'Flannagain chief was one of the royal lords of the King of Connaught. The family motto is 'I have fought and conquered'. I sent the card to Barry.

In the autumn of 2007 Barry came to London with Jessica. We had dinner together in a Chinese restaurant in the East End and then talked into the early hours at the studio flat he kept above the foundry. Barry seemed in excellent spirits. There was no sign of the irritability of yore and his life seemed on an even keel both domestically and professionally. He looked well physically. He had put on a bit of weight but it suited him. I mentioned my new partner and added she was from Iran. A few days later Jessica rang and said Barry had proposed we all to go to a Persian restaurant in Convent Garden. Everybody liked the food and belly dancing, and we drank Château Musar, a robust and exquisite red wine from Lebanon.

About a year later Barry rang. He was in London and, by way of reciprocation, we invited him and Jessica to another Persian restaurant we knew on the Harrow Road, which with its sumptuous décor and baked-on-the-premises flat bread almost transported you to Tehran. On the phone Barry sounded hoarse and wheezed as he spoke. He told me he was not feeling very well. He had always had a tendency to whisper but this seemed different. I assumed it might have something to do with smoking and even thought it could be emphysema. I mentioned that after a long battle I had given up tobacco and one thing that had helped had been sucking on crystallized ginger, which mimicked the sensation of inhaling and was good for the health in general. I told him where he could get some.

Despite his poor throat, we arranged to meet at Groucho's, from where we would go on to the restaurant. Unfortunately, my partner and I both went down with flu and had to cancel. Barry took this cheerfully on the phone but by now was wheezing so badly I could hardly hear him. On November 25 he copied me into an email he sent to Galerie Lelong in Paris, who were now handling all his non-

sculptural work. After mentioning the Ibiza show and his desire that it should be properly placed in his chronology, he brought up the piece he had given the museum in Ibiza, *Head of the Goddess*:

> *In celebration of a birth I gave them the torso*
> *of the mother mounted on an original base,*
> *with the (also bronze) head of an infant, placed*
> *on a book of Poetry by Antonio Colinas*
> *Open at a certain page.*
>
> *May I c/c Richard so he may give you details.*
> *I would like this v. Much.*
>
> *If in the fullness of time the Museum would*
> *Release the Work an edition can be made &*
> *We could see that most modest of Museums Benefit.*

It was typical of Barry, who had written on his wall 'I am an artist, I am an artist and think only of myself' (there is some dispute about this, but I have a vivid recollection of seeing this) to be so concerned about the wellbeing of others, in this case the museum on Ibiza. I heard no more about this and on 26 March 2009 sent him an email in which I asked if he would like me to provide him with material I had relating to the Ibiza show of 1992. I also expressed my hope that his chest problem had cleared up. On 6 April I received this reply:

> Thanks for the thought, Richard.
> In fact it is Motor Neuron Disease.
> I have a PowerChair for mobility
> and need Nursing.
> It will be great if you send your
> dated writings.

A few hours later he sent me another mail, which led to me meeting up with his artistic executor Jo Melvin, to whom I gave copies of all my writings connected with the Ibiza show. I heard from her that his form of the disease was incurable and incredibly fast-acting. It had attacked his trachea thereby jeopardizing his ability to eat, breathe and speak. He had actually been forced to give up the last and now communicated by writing notes. He had reacted with understandable fury to the diagnosis and the prognosis was not good. As I later heard from Ab, he had been given 'five to fifteen', which the foundry boss took at that time to mean years but later realized were months. Jo, however, had been to see him on Ibiza and, as much as anyone in his situation could, he seemed to be coming to terms with things. I told her I would visit him as well. In the meantime, there was a spate of activity surrounding Barry's work, including an exhibition called Hare Coursed at the New Art Gallery near Salisbury in May. Two coaches collected about a hundred people from outside Tate Britain one wet Saturday morning and took us down there.

The sculpture park at Roche Court, home of the New Art Gallery, is unusual in that there are no works on plinths and the sculptures are placed almost at random in the rolling Wiltshire countryside. Such an arrangement suited the several hares on display as well as the intriguing bishops I had first seen in Dublin, now placed to either side of a summerhouse. There was a soft rain falling and the galleries within the house had on show early pieces in canvas, Tuscan stone and hessian, as well as drawings of nudes and landscapes executed with Barry's remarkable line. No matter how well you knew his work there were always fresh surprises – for me, the chess set in the upstairs gallery with pieces made of inevitably green stuffed fabric. Nearby, there was a recent film of Barry, Jessica and Alfred on a wide sunny terrace I did not recognize. Barry was in his power chair. He had lost a considerable amount of weight and was wearing a kimono and hat. He smiled for the camera but in his eyes I saw an expression I could only describe as stricken.

A month later I was in Santa Eulalia looking into those same piercing, hazel-flecked eyes. There was a more resigned expression in them now, and he seemed proud of his mastery of the power chair, which had brought him out into the living room to greet me. Outside was the wide terrace of the recently acquired flat I had seen in the film, which looked out onto roofs and then the marina, bristling with the masts of the yachts. We went into the kitchen and he offered me a glass of strong molasses-like sherry. A few months before I had built a website, which included a section dedicated to my mother's poems and paintings. Barry had called the site 'commendably clear' and asked if I would like to take a bottle of the same sherry back for her. He did this in note form and seemed to have mastered the art of writing precise, economical phrases. Before he became ill he and Jessica had visited Goa. He wrote 'You been?' I mentioned the unholy trinity of my youth – Ibiza, Amsterdam, Goa – of which I only spent time in the first two because I thought the last might be too wild and hedonistic for my taste. 'Me too,' he wrote.

We went for a walk to the marina with Jessica and I trying to keep up. Barry had taken to his motorized wheelchair with gusto and it was a common sight to see him whizzing around the streets of the pueblo. We stopped beside an empty berth. Barry had a bag of bread with him and fed the large grey fish that slid over each other in a feeding frenzy, trying to get at the pieces. On the way back to the flat Jessica bought ice cream. Barry had a little tub of a blueberry flavoured one that was soft on his throat. He was focusing a lot on diet, Jessica told me, as we sat later at a table in the café alongside their block, Barry having gone up to the apartment. He had been given three months, she said, but almost double that time had passed since. It seemed that Barry had a very high metal content in his body. This was strange when you considered most of the work involving contact with metal was delegated to others. Also, apart from bronze, he had made things principally from soft materials such as felt and sackcloth. The metal had not obviously come from his work unless from when he was starting out. He was on a special diet designed to detox him, with foods such as an unusual type of mushrooms, that the hope was would stop the illness spreading from his trachea to his lungs.

During this visit, I went into Ibiza town to see Elena. Our appointment was at eleven but reaching the museum I found the tall front doors closed. Wondering if she had forgotten, I walked round the back. The entire area behind the museum was one vast building site. I approached one of the workmen and he told me Elena was probably in the council building further up in Dalt Vila where the museum had been temporarily housed during the renovations. I walked up there but Elena was not to be found, though *Head of the Goddess* was. It was the first sight that greeted visitors to the small exhibition of pieces from the museum's collection displayed in two medium-sized rooms on the ground floor. The statue had been placed before a light red background. The torso was no longer gilded but had returned to the shades of its original bronze. The book, always the most expendable part of the assembly, had a tattered appearance and a couple of pages had detached themselves from the spine.

The woman at the desk told me Elena was in fact at the Puget Museum, a short walk away. This turned out to be a handsome building built in gothic style with Catalan influence, the oldest part of which dates back to the fifteenth century. Reached via a wide and elegant stone staircase are a set of galleries that exhibit paintings and watercolours by two artists from the Puget family. I found Elena in a well-equipped office. I had last called on her in 2005 and as then she seemed little changed from the eager curator of the early 1990s, except that her hair was seamed by silver. She told me she did not know how long she would be using this temporary office. During the renovation of the museum the workmen had come upon Punic remains. It was a fascinating discovery but had placed a big question mark over the museum's reopening date, as the remains would have to be properly excavated and preserved. She asked about Barry and I told her what was wrong with him, which she had not known. Then I mentioned that I had seen *Head of the Goddess* in the temporary exhibition in the council building. She said they had brought Barry there a few weeks earlier and placed his wheelchair before his sculpture. He had taken a long look at the torso and the book and burst into tears.

During my visit I shared the lift in Barry's building with his son. Alfred was trying to remember some lines of poetry he wanted to say to his father. He recited a couple of words and I realized it was Dylan Thomas's 'Do Not Go Gentle Into That Good Night'. The poet, of course, had written the lines for his own father and they seemed noble words to repeat. When we found Barry, however, he was peacefully watching tennis on the television, only the power chair and his shrinking frame testifying to anything amiss. Indeed, the resoluteness and courage he displayed in the face of terrible adversity was remarkable. Not once did I see a flicker of self-pity, and his consideration for others never faltered for a moment. Yet as his capacities dwindled with cruel rapidity, Barry did 'rage against the dying of the light'.

In the relatively few months from the inception of the disease to its conclusion, the sculptor remained remarkably active, albeit often inevitably at one remove. Loans became gifts; plans for the archive were finalized; there was the Salisbury show and the unveiling of *Large Mirror Nijinski* (1992) outside the headquarters of the British Council on the Mall in London. The filmmaker Peter Bach recorded the last two occasions in a work called *Flanagan's Wake*, the main thrust of which was to film Barry's public sculptures in different countries – the enigmatic *Vizitor* (1989), in Les Halles, Paris, or the hare in the coastal dunes on the Belgian/Dutch border – and get local reactions to them. Parts of the film show Barry taking in Bach's production. There is childlike delight on his face when an archivist in Washington DC describes how his *Thinker on a Rock* was Hillary Clinton's favourite when she paid a visit to the city's National Gallery of Art and Sculpture. Barry's sense of humour has not deserted him nor his rebellious spirit such as when he writes, 'The day the Arts Council sported a logo it was all over.' More sombrely we see him at a table digging into a ball of wet clay with his thumb in order to hollow out the centre and produce a pinch pot. Occasionally, he pauses from the modelling to write in a notebook. He has got to the place you find in Beckett plays were there is no time for the superfluous, just the bare bones in the face of death. He writes of his growing weakness, the difficulty he is having in making an impression on the clay. He draws a line under these words, as though needing to compartmentalize each thought before he can move on to the next one. Then he writes 'Impossible'. He returns to hollowing out the clay but his fingers lack the strength to do so properly. Raising the moist pot with both hands, he hurls it facedown against the page in the notebook, to which it sticks.

At another point in the film, Barry describes making pinch pots as the closest he has come to prayer: 'a physical mantra'. The cover of the first volume of *Silâns*, the magazine of Barry's youth, begins with a quote from Joyce's *Ulysses* that uses the onomatopoeic sound of a printing press, 'Sllt', to make the point that 'Everything speaks in its own way' – and Barry has always known how to listen to things. But now everything is falling silent, the mantra is over, and there is just unimaginable loss. Who would not rage?

The last time I saw Barry was at the Pomelo. I got him a vodka with peach juice and shook his hand when we said goodbye, noticing the large liver blotches on its surface that were just like Monica's. 'Till we meet,' I said, hoping more than anything else that this would be true. The last thing I heard from him was in an email dated 4 July 2009. He wrote:

> Just to let you know Elena has arranged a big interview,
> tell her I think you should be part of it.

The interview was to be with a Spanish newspaper, *Ultima Hora*, but Barry was not well enough to do it.

Also in July I received an email from the publisher Alexandra Pringle, who worked for Barry as a personal assistant in the late 1970s and early 1980s, and had just returned from visiting him in Santa Eulalia. She said he had asked her to read to him one of the dated writings I had sent, an unpublished piece about the Ibiza show. They had both rolled about with laughter, she informed me. I was pleased to hear that something I had made provided a bridge in what could have been an awkward reunion, given his silence and the time that had elapsed.

# 23

I REACHED THE church about ten o'clock: the Puig d'en Missa in Santa Eulalia, whose thick white walls sat like icing on the red, summer-baked earth. I was still a bit dazed, having caught a late flight riotous with partygoers, whose boisterous anticipation of the days of sun and sex ahead was quite at odds with my own mood. I had then snatched about four hours' sleep. The road up to the church had been steep and I was sweating. The service was not due to begin for another hour but there were already several people gathered outside.

The church had been built in the sixteenth century on a hill overlooking the road from Ibiza town on one side, and Santa Eulalia on the other, in order to protect it from pirates. Despite the heat and sunlight, there was a hint of closeness in the air that presaged the sequence of storms with which summer in the Balearics ends. Some of those mingling on the steps or sitting on the walls wore black, others ordinary dress. It did not really matter. After a while, with the doors remaining shut and no sign of a priest, there was speculation that the service would be held outside, a hiccup many felt Barry would have appreciated. A few minutes after eleven, however, two priests in white vestments showed up, both from the English community. The doors were opened, and about two hundred people filed into the church as a girl played the guitar and sang just beside the entrance. It was 11 September 2009. Barry had died on 31 August in the Rosario clinic in Ibiza town.

After prayers and a hymn, Jessica read 'Head of the Goddess in my Hands'. She recited the poem in Spanish. An English translation was printed in the booklet that contained the order of service. If the reading was in English, it was done the other way round and a translation in Spanish was provided. Enrique Juncosa's eulogy, however, which was not printed, he made in one language and then the other. In it he mapped the key points of the sculptor's career. After this a barefoot Flan went to the rostrum and read 'Concerning the Surface of God', Jarry's 'pataphysical description of a supreme being, which after a number of precise measurements enigmatically concludes that, 'God is the shortest distance between zero and infinity.'

In 1998 Barry had collaborated with Hugh Cornwell on a recording of a poem called 'Mantra of the Awoken Powers' by Sex W. Johnston. The poem, which deals with the death of a brother, struck a chord with Barry and his delivery is memorable and heartfelt. Cornwell had provided a musical backing that fitted perfectly. There had been a single public performance at Whelan's Bar, Dublin. Initially, the punkish audience, attracted by Cornwell's reputation as a former Strangler, had greeted the appearance of Barry, attired in a tweed suit and heavy woollen scarf, with cries of 'Go home, grandpa!' They had, however, quickly been won over by the sincerity of Barry's recitation and the power of Cornwell's riff and had gone berserk at the end. When the piece came to be recorded, some 'pataphysical gremlins intruded and the sculptor ended up reciting the poem down an answer phone. 'Mantra of the Awoken Powers' was played next, to the further consternation of clergy still mulling over Jarry's definition of God, though its last line 'and I remain while he remaineth not' sounded pretty biblical to me.

After this I read the Lesson, the famous passage from Ecclesiastes: 'There is a time for everything and a season for every activity under heaven: a time to be born and a time to die...' As I made my way back to my seat, I thought of the device Jarry had proposed

in 'Practical Construction of a Time Machine' with enough detail and sophistication to have it taken seriously by several scientists. Where would Barry have gone back to if he could have used it? To the Silver Jubilee Exhibition in Battersea Park and the prankster impulse that prompted him to place a small turd-shaped stone behind the rear end of Henry Moore's *Sheep Piece* (1971-72)? To receiving his OBE from the Queen when she said, 'You make big pieces,' and he had replied, 'Fortunately, Ma'am'? To the moment he saw a hare bounding across the Sussex Downs and the idea struck him?

Alternatively, setting the controls to the future, the time machine could have travelled to that day in late January of the following year when I visited the foundry by the Limehouse Cut and watched Mark Jones work on the bronze bust of a woman with a Nijinski hare balanced on her shoulder. Other productions of Barry's final period stood alongside Mark's work table. There was a bronze of a woman with a halo-like garland in her hair whose prototype I had seen on Ibiza when I stayed with Barry. A sculpture of Jessica sitting on a rock, the face a perfect likeness, and a homage to the Venus de Milo with features like Annabelle's. All were in bronze and suggested that Barry, had he lived, might have taken an increasingly classical path, one focused on veneration of the female, though as ever the sculptor resisted pigeonholing and other late work, such as *Moulded Tower* (2005), and *Direct Tower* (2005), suggest he was intent on reproducing the shapes and texture of his early hessian work in more durable bronze. Apart from Barry's work there were numerous editions of a sculpture of the model Kate Moss in yoga positions in the room. These were by Marc Quinn, who had worked as Barry's assistant in 1983.

Back in church the priest giving the sermon seemed to have been a bit unsettled by Alfred Jarry. This new definition of God would certainly give him pause for thought, he told us before speaking of Barry and of loss. There was another hymn and then we filed out into the full glare of noon. All sorts of people were milling about including those who had come down from London for the occasion, such as Leslie Waddington and Ab from the foundry.

Catherine Lampert, director of the Whitechapel Art Gallery when Barceló had had his show was also there. When I spoke to her, I found that, as with me, her dealings with Barry had not always been smooth sailing. She hints at this in the obituary she wrote for *The Guardian* when she describes the 'English-speaking itinerant European sculptor' in his last years 'wavering between a desire to computerize his records and sort out his legacy and a need for control.' Other obituaries described him as 'Britain's best-known and most controversial modernist' (*The Daily Telegraph*) and 'one of the most versatile, imaginative and radical sculptors of his generation' (*The Independent*). More poignant were the comments and 'warm amen' to the obituaries posted on the Internet, which were replicated in September 2011 when an article of mine appeared in *The Guardian* to coincide with the opening of the show of Barry's early work at Tate Britain. A comment Ronnie Wood left in the early hours of the morning was sadly deemed inappropriate but a post by someone else recalled attending a guest lecture Barry gave as 'a wonderful experience in the sense of a good pub session with a stranger that stays with you forever.' Part of Barry's legacy is the gratitude he left in the hearts of the many he inspired or gave a leg up to with unstinting generosity. He was someone who enhanced both his surroundings and those around him, not just with works of indelible wit and beauty, but also with deeds dictated by the heart.

Another person present was Miquel Barceló, now renowned among other things for his extraordinary contribution to Palma cathedral, the Chapel of Saint Peter, an environment themed around the biblical story of the feeding of the 10,000, totally rendered out of ceramic clay. When we spoke in Barry's garden later, he seemed little changed from the vibrant individual I had first met seventeen years before. He told me Barry had visited him again on Mallorca for *matanzas* (pig killings). Many people from the expat community were present and I saw Helga, widow of Martin Watson Todd, and Leon Dupont, who had published Martin's poetry. I told them there were to be some readings back at the big house and the family had asked me to MC the occasion. Helga and Leon said I should read the poem Martin had written about Barry, which was called 'Games'. I told them the same thought had crossed my mind.

At the house we gave a reading in the garden near a shrine to Barry, an urn containing his ashes surrounded by flowers, candles and a photo. Anu, who had worked for Barry on Ibiza for many years, started things off by talking amusingly about the sculptor and Flanaganese. I said a few words then recited Martin's poem:

> This man will play games with you
> But your act better be good.
> Disconcerting when he is the window
> And the wall you beat your head on.
> He don't give a fuck about full stops and agony,
> He ain't interested in your flowers,
> He sees you, you who see the wall, the window,
> And the view of the sea you think is limitless.
>
> But what is unbearable will be
> The paper bag you put the rubbish in.
> We could go on about the difficulties,
> But he says get the beer, just so,
> And do you speak Swahili?

*If you want to push it further*
*You'll find him behind you, laughing.*

*You might think he's laughing at you —*
*Reason has the face of an anonymous stone.*
*But is it reasonable that on this beach of stones*
*You'll find one that speaks only to you?*
*I'm afraid you'll have to forget the sea*
*If you want to see the stones beneath your feet.*
*If you want to be a master, end this poem.*
*No clues! I'm waiting to embrace you, Friend.*

It is hard in its way, but there you have it. Barry had his fury and a salamander fire with which he would happily roast those who patronized him or were short on the consideration for others by which he placed such store. 'Draw a straight line between civility and survival,' as he told the wall one day. He liked playing games and testing people. He has become his admirers and other editions will appear. If they wash away the grit, they may not find the pearl.

Other speakers followed: Barry's long-time friend Kevin Whitney; Jo Melvin, who recited Phillip King's 'Prayer for Drawing'; Robin Marchesi, who read extracts from the passages Barry had dictated to him throughout their association. Then Alexandra Pringle introduced the piece I had written about the Ibiza show. She described how Barry had asked her to read it to him and how everything about his reaction — 'Did I really do that? Was that really me?' — had expressed his delight. After my reading, Alfred got up and spoke movingly about his dad. Alfred had been a remarkable child, a natural 'pataphysician from an early age with an original view of things, as well as a very sharp one. Once, when travelling with his father, a customs officer had asked the boy, who must have been about seven or eight at the time, if the itinerant sculptor was his father. 'Sometimes,' Alfred replied.

We had arranged to end it there and that seemed fitting. There would be other memorial events: at the Royal Academy in November 2009 and in Dublin in January 2010. But after her brother had finished Annabelle unexpectedly got up and went and stood next to him. Then she turned her lovely face in our direction and began to speak of the

OPPOSITE
*Alfred Jarry loves Rrose Sélavy*, 1974,
Pen on paper,
9 3/4" x 7 5/8" /
24.8cm x 19.4cm

thousand things that die each second, plants, and blades of grass, and animals, without anything or anybody caring. Yet human death is an affliction to others. She spoke of being at the hospital with her dad, holding his hand as he began to fade with Jessica holding the other. Of how he had delivered her, alone with Renate, and witnessed her first breath while she was there when he drew his last.

*Head of the Goddess in my Hands*

*Cabeza de la diosa entre mis manos*

654 a.C.

Barro oscuro conforma tu figura
que mantiene el tiempo detenido.
Ser hombre o ser dios hoy es lo mismo:
sólo un poco de tierra humedecida
a la que un sol antiguo dio dureza,
hermosura mortal, luz muy madura.
Pero lo que ha durado esta cabeza
frágil que ha contemplado tantos siglos
la muerte de los otros, que en mis manos
descansa, se hace fugazmente eterno.
En su rostro moreno cae la noche,
cae mucha luz de ocaso en sus dos labios
y cae un día más de nuestra vida.
Misterio superior este de ver
cómo su cuerpo acumula siglos
mientras el nuestro pierde juventud.
Misterio de dos barros que han brotado
de un mismo pozo y bajo un mismo fuego.
Mas sólo a uno de ellos concedió
el Arte la virtud de ser divino
y, en consecuencia, no morir jamás.

Antonio Colinas

# FURTHER READING

'In Appreciation', obituary of Barry that appeared in *Ibiza Now* October
2009: can be found on www.richardmcneff.co.uk.
'Barry Flanagan exhibits on Ibiza', *Boulevard Magenta*, IV
(Irish Museum of Modern Art: Dublin 2011).
'Barry Flanagan at Tate: Hare Today, but not Gone Tomorrow': article in
*The Guardian* that coincided with the opening of Barry Flanagan: Early
Works 1965–1982 at Tate Britain (26 September 2011–2 January
2012). www.guardian.co.uk/artanddesign/2011/sep/26/barry-
flanagan-tate-britain-exhibition
Enrique Juncosa and Richard McNeff, *Miquel Barceló i Barry Flanagan.
Ceràmiques i Dibuxos* (MACE, Ajuntament D'Eivissa, Ibiza 2012)

# REFERENCES

*We Love You* (Booth-Clibborn Editions / Candy Records: London 1998).
Cohen, J.M (ed.), *The Penguin Book of Spanish Verse* (Penguin: London
1988).
Colinas, Antonio, *Los Días en la Isla*, (Huerga y Fierro editores, S.L.:
Madrid 2004).
*En L'Esperit De Fluxus*, (Fundació Antoni Tàpies: 1994).
Ewart Evans, George and Thomson, David, *The Leaping Hare* (Faber:
London 1973).
Flanagan, Barry, *Catalogue to the Madrid Retrospective 1993*, ed. Alexandra
Pringle 1941–81, Clarrie Rudrum 1982–93 (Fundación La Caixa
with the British Council: 1993).
Flanagan, Barry and Floris, Marcel, *Catalogue* (Museu d'Art
Contemporani d'Eivissa: 1992).
*Barry Flanagan: Early Works 1965–1982*, eds. Clarrie Wallis and Andrew
Wilson (Tate Publishing: London 2011).
Jarry, Alfred, *Adventures in 'Pataphysics: Collected Works I* (Atlas Press:
London 2001).
Jarry, Alfred, *Exploits and Opinions of Dr Faustroll, 'Pataphysician* (Exact
Change: Boston 1996).
Marchesi, Robin, *Barry Flanagan: Poet of the Building Site* (Irish Museum
of Modern Art/Edizioni Charta: Milano 2011).
Melvin, Jo, *Barry Flanagan (Works 1966–2008)* (Waddington Galleries:
London 2010).
Melvin, Jo (editor), *Silâns 1964–65*, Plubronze Limited (Lethaby Press:
2011).
Miles, Barry, *London Calling: a Countercultural History of London Since 1945*

(Atlantic Books: London 2010).

Paul, Elliot, *The Life and Death of a Spanish Town* (Random House: New York 1937).

Richardson, Paul, *Not Part of the Package: a Year on Ibiza* (Macmillan: London 1992).

Shattuck, Roger, *The Banquet Years: the Origins of the Avant-Garde in France, 1885 to World War I* (Vintage: London 1958).

Watson Todd, Martin, *Poems* (Leon Dupont: Amsterdam 1992)

The Archive of Barry Flanagan

## ARTICLES

Victoria Combalía, 'Artefactos Serios – Las dos etapas estilísticas del escultor Barry Flanagan', *El País* (19 September 1992).

Helen Delaney, 'Rope (Gr 2Sp 60) 6 '67, *Tate Collection* (September 2002).

Chrissie Iles, 'On John Latham', *Art Forum* (2006).

John McEwen, 'Take one stiff hare and a dog-biscuit factory', *The Sunday Telegraph* (13 June 1993).

Tom Overton, 'Barry Flanagan Venice Biennale Participation', (www.britishcouncil.org).

Vicent Tur, 'Barry Flanagan y Marcel Floris Exponen en el MAC', *Diario de Ibiza* (3 June 1992).

## A NOTE ON THE AUTHOR

Richard McNeff was born in London but lived all over Britain as a child. His father was a repertory theatre actor who subsequently went into film and television. His mother is a poet. After reading English at Sussex University, Richard worked as a carpenter and wrote stories for *International Times*. He subsequently lived in Barcelona, Amsterdam, the Basque country and Baku, settling on Ibiza where he stayed for several years. He currently lives in London. Articles and reviews by him have appeared in *Fortean Times*, *Boulevard Magenta* and *The Guardian*. His novel, *Sybarite among the Shadows*, is a tale of spies and magic set in London's bohemia of the 1930s.